A Tissue in Every Pocket

☙

Karen Desrosiers

Purple World Publishing • Exeter, NH

For Devlin

The love of my life and my reason for being.

Purple World Publishing, Exeter, NH

www.karendesrosiers.com

Available from author, Amazon.com, and other retailers.

Table of Contents

Introduction

CB

At the beginning of 1997, I found myself in a foreign, frightening, and utterly overwhelming situation. Within the span of a month, I gave birth to a beautiful baby boy, Dev, finalized my divorce, and became a single mother. Dreams held dear since adolescence simultaneously came true and evaporated into fog. I had the child I had always longed for but not the husband I assumed would be there by my side through it all. I was *solely* responsible for another human, one who was completely defenseless and dependent on me. While I had family support readily available, as well as the support of friends, I had marched into parenthood alone.

Despite the stories we hear, the parents we know, and the advice we receive, I don't think anyone is ever fully prepared for how absolutely and completely life changes once you have a child. Until you're there, you can't truly imagine it.

For most of us, when we envisioned having children, we instinctually knew the reward would far outweigh the sacrifice; we took it on faith that the joy would dwarf the struggle, and we had the reassurance (in our dreams at least) that when parenthood came, we would not be going through it alone. In the world I grew up in, it seemed to be a universally given understanding that, for couples, having a child would be a glorious experience that we would share and that would enrich our relationship with our partner or spouse.

Reality, I've found, rarely matches the imagination or expectation. Life most often fails to live up to the dream. The childhood fantasy of growing up to have a picture-perfect family doesn't happen just because we hoped it would. Many people end up becoming single parents, though I suspect many had likely never predicted that would be the case.

Most aspects of parenthood are common and universal, whether you are a single parent, co-parent, or married, with boys or girls, one child or many. However, there are many perspectives and aspects of parenting that are unique for the single-parent and perhaps some that are particularly unique for a single mother of a boy.

Dev and I were on our own from day one, just the two of us. Thankfully, we had tremendous support from family and friends along the way, and because of that, we have never been, and will never be, totally alone. But our family unit has always been mother and son, and that has always been fine with us. He's never questioned it, and I've never regretted it. This is how it was meant to be.

I started writing, long before Dev came into my life. As I forged a life for us, writing became a way for me to process, vent about, and document our lives and experiences. In January 2001, I began writing a column on single parenting called "On Our Own" for *Our Times*, a monthly women's magazine published by the Seacoast Media Group in Portsmouth, New Hampshire. Through that monthly column, I was able to debrief and explore aspects of our life together, from teaching my son how to stand-up pee, to his first sleep over, from peaceful mornings alone, to the question of buying a dad. Many of the essays that I've gathered here were originally printed as columns for "On Our Own." I have also included a number of essays that were not previously published. The essays are organized (for the most part) in chronological order, starting when Dev was an infant, though this is not necessarily the order in which they were all written.

I hope that everyone reading these essays will find a situation to relate to, a nugget to laugh with, and a lesson to learn from. These are just a few stories of life between a mom and young son. Enjoy.

On Becoming a Single Parent

☙

I have always wanted to be a mother. I don't remember there ever being a time when I didn't long for a truck-load of children. Most of my life has been spent dreaming about days filled with laughter, corralling five small boys — I've always wanted five, and I've always wanted boys. I imagined listening to the shouts and giggles as my own little crew played tag and hide-n-seek in the yard. I pictured little bodies covered with mud and grass stains, searching for hugs and Popsicles. I wanted a family, husband and children, but the children were the primary treasure I sought. From early on, I knew I was prepared to choose single motherhood, if necessary, as a means of reaching this goal, though I hoped it wouldn't come to that. I wanted children more than anything else in my life.

The right man and marriage stubbornly eluded me. As

my thirtieth birthday came and went, finding me still single, I decided that I would have to take matters firmly in my own capable hands. It was time to end the waiting and wanting, time for action.

I moved to a more desirable area, fleeing suburban chaos for a small town and good school district. I wanted a yard for my child or children to run in, a neighborhood playground, and a short drive to the beach. Intent on reaching independence, I launched my own business. It was clear that I would need the flexibility of self-employment if I were a single parent.

Little by little, I began collecting soft baby outfits in beautiful shades of green, yellow, and blue. I bought a traditional cedar hope chest. Instead of filling it with linens, candle holders, towels, and negligées, as a hopeful bride might, I filled it with stuffed animals, blankets, little one-piece pajamas with attached feet, and baby food cookbooks. With each passing month, I looked through the contents of the chest, mentally taking stock and making notes of what else I might want. I found some beautiful t-shirts, hand painted with a frog, puppy, and bunny, and bought them, folding them neatly and stowing them securely in the cedar chest.

When my new business was well underway, and I was nearing thirty-three, it was time to move forward with the dream of becoming a mother. I made a chart of all the men I knew, carefully laying out their strengths and weaknesses, personalities, talents, physical traits, tastes, and hobbies, as well as noting any annoying habits that I imagined could be passed down to a child. I read over the list repeatedly, evaluating each entry for his suitability as a potential father, weighing the pros and cons of each the way one might compare features in *Consumer Reports* when buying a new car.

Next, I searched out sperm banks, investigating quality, price, and variety, reading the testimonials like they were gospel. My favorites were the services that offered an online, searchable database of donors. Performing query after query, I searched by ancestral nationality, eye color, career, and preferred pastimes. The variety of services being offered was also amazing, including one company that sold a "do-it-yourself" kit that promised a discreet box with the desired specimen and "easy to use" inseminator, which I could only visualize as a turkey baster.

I made another chart and weighed the merits of a known versus anonymous donor. There were clear advantages to the anonymous donor avenue. For one thing, I could practically design the child I wanted — choosing hair and eye color, height, ethnicity, and possible interests, though I was concerned that possible annoying habits weren't disclosed. I considered Celtic features to match my own or a more exotic look. I wasn't limited to the small circle of potential donors I knew — there was a whole world of men out there who had chosen to contribute. The aspects of complete privacy and autonomy also appealed to me. There would be a very slim chance that the baby would look like anyone I knew, so potential guessing-games over who the father was might be kept to a minimum.

On the other hand, using a known donor would certainly be more affordable. A known donor also opened up the possibility that the baby might get to know his or her father, if we wanted that door to be open. It would certainly be easier to tell the child about his father rather than having to say I didn't know who the father was because all I met was a numbered test tube that arrived at the door in a discreet cooler, with a baster.

Issues of religious conviction crossed my mind countless times. Having been raised Roman Catholic, no matter what choice I made, intentionally becoming a single mother by any means or methods outside of marriage was not exactly acceptable. It wasn't that this would be an issue within my own spirituality, but I worried this could be difficult for some of my family. I resolved that I would spend the rest of my life asking for forgiveness if I had to, confident that in the light of bringing a new baby into the family I would receive it.

I discussed my plans with a select few people. Not everyone would be open to this tactic, I knew, and it would be better to tell them after the baby was well under way, when there was no longer a risk of being talked out of it. Those who I did confide in were both surprised and supportive, helping to bolster my resolve that this was the right choice, the right direction for my life.

Then, the unthinkable happened, something wholly unexpected. Just as I reached the point of making final decisions about how to proceed, I met someone. And, even more amazingly, he seemed like the right someone. His caring spirit and ability to cook were balanced with an adventurous nature. He had the sense of humor and heart-felt laugh that I had always fantasized my brood of boys would have.

I tucked my research into a folder and put my plans for single-parenthood aside. I longed for a baby, but if there was the possibility of having a child with someone, it was worth giving it some time. I deserved that. My future child deserved that.

One of the first matters of discussion in my new relationship was the possibility of children — in the future. I was thrilled to find that he loved children as much as I did. He was ready for a family, he assured me. We spent many afternoons, sipping coffee and casually discussing what our children might look like, how many we would have, and how quickly. I watched happily as he played with the kids we knew, secure in the thought that I could share children with him.

When we married, I immediately began my prayers for a child. We had agreed children would be "later", but I was ready and didn't want to wait. I had a "donor" right there, day in and day out; it was my chance. Even after the marriage soured, a mere three months later, I prayed for a baby. The marriage continued to deteriorate quickly and slipped into a dangerous pattern of emotional and verbal abuse, but I continued to hope for a child.

A little more than a year into a marriage that wasn't working, as I struggled to decide whether or not to leave him, I got pregnant. I found myself once again faced with the possibility of becoming a single mother — for real, not just in a chart on paper. There was a choice to be made: bring a child into an abusive marriage or become a single parent.

The news of my pregnancy was not met with the joy and pride one might expect from a husband who had previously dreamed about a future with children, or at least had said he did. The news was not welcome or accepted in any way. Overwhelmed with disappointment and heartache, but also motivated, I packed my bags and moved out.

My dream to have a child was being realized, and I was about to become a mother. It had happened within the bond of marriage, but the marriage would not survive. The marriage could be annulled, but the baby could not be returned.

Nine months later, still groggy from the pain medication after a cesarean birth, I gingerly propped myself up in my hospital bed. A nurse wheeled a plastic bassinet into the room. I held my breath as she lifted a compact bundle of blanket and curly black hair from the bed.

"There you are," I said and reached my hands out toward the nurse. "There's my boy."

She placed my new son into my arms, and my eyes locked with his. The first of my brood, I thought, finally. Holding him close to my heart, I draped his small fingers over mine and rubbed my cheek against his. He was perfect and sweet. I knew that I would be content with him, just the two of us, even if he ended up a brood of one.

Empowerment

❦

We live in a society of buzzwords and popular terms. They come, and they go, with the latest fad in self-help, business management, and technological development. By the time you finish your morning coffee, a handful of words that were mundane and obscure pieces of vocabulary yesterday may have become buzzwords today. Empowerment is one such word.

According to a number of dictionaries, empowerment is an authority or power that is officially or legally granted to a person. However, in our society, empowerment seems to have become a quality we earn through conviction and action. I've heard people say that they've been empowered by a song they heard, a poem they read, or a documentary they watched. Some people seem to be empowered by witnessing the brave and heroic actions of others, while some feel that empowerment is a birthright, neither earned nor achieved.

I continually struggle with this elusive quality. I have taken many risks, enjoyed successes, and suffered losses. I have traveled internationally by myself and dined alone in expensive restaurants. I married a virtual stranger, in an exotic foreign land, and survived an abusive marriage. I left a secure job, with a healthy income, to start several businesses, some of which failed, while some succeeded. All of these risks and actions I've taken out of stubborn determination, yet none have left me feeling empowered. I felt strong, yes, and independent for sure, but bestowed with power and authority, no. I still woke up every morning, directionless and ineffective, wondering if I could make it through the day, the week.

I began to wonder if empowerment really was only a trendy buzzword, with no tie to any concrete feelings or experiences, with no tie to reality. What did it actually mean? How could I get it? Who had the right and ability to grant empowerment, to me or anyone else? Would I have to attend some assertiveness training class to find the key to this allusive force? Was there a self-help book available that would show the way to develop it on my own schedule?

Giving birth, I had been told, was the most empowering experience a woman could have, especially if she could make it through labor without the help of sensation-deadening drugs. I had a cesarean birth, which did not leave me feeling at all empowered. My body did not do its job. I did not go into labor, I did not even dilate, and I was not able to deliver my child as nature intended. Don't get me wrong; I'm not bitter, resentful, or disappointed about my experience. Many women have cesareans, and it does not diminish or devalue the process of becoming a mother. I had a beautiful, healthy son, and we both came through the experience safely. It just did not confer me with any sense of power, not even a hint.

These thoughts would hit me at nine in the morning, while I enjoyed my coffee and a bowl of granola, and my infant son peacefully napped not ten feet away. I had made it through another sleepless night, singing the ABC's at one, offering a painful breast to my ravenous child at three thirty. It was then, ironically energized by my lack of sleep, that I realized I had finally been empowered. Somehow, at some point — I hadn't even noticed when it happened — power, confidence, and authority had found me on their own, seeping into my weary muscles.

I survived feedings every two hours around the clock. I made it through Dev's first fever, first ear infection, and hours of whining before his first tooth broke through. We dealt with a congenital hip defect that dictated he wear a brace on his legs for his first four months of life. We endured stomach bugs, the worst allergy season in five years, eczema, and head bumps while Dev learned to sit up. Against all the odds, I survived the first six months of being a single parent.

To top it off, I did it all without getting evicted from our apartment. I managed to work, pay the rent, keep the utilities turned on and dishes washed, buy the diapers, and change them as well. It wasn't easy. Sleep deprivation is a serious problem. One morning, I put two contacts in my right eye and couldn't figure out why everything was blurry. I developed a frustrating habit of putting the cereal box in the refrigerator and the milk in the cabinet. And I had to write everything down because my short-term memory went on strike, with no promise it would return.

I won't say I did it all by myself. I could never have survived completely alone. Dev and I spent the first month of his life at my parents' house. I took care of my son; my mother took care of me. As it was, I could barely move for the first couple of weeks and was completely incapable of preparing food for myself. I would never have managed to take care of us both, especially not with the fabulous painkillers they had given me after the cesarean surgery.

When Dev was about five months old, I had the opportunity to pursue a relationship. An acquaintance was interested in spending more time together, perhaps getting closer. Not a year earlier I would have jumped at the chance to be in a serious relationship, to not be alone. But everything had changed with the birth of my son. I bowed out gracefully, saying I didn't have the time, but thinking I really didn't have the need or interest.

When I looked at my son, as he sat on the living room floor and his two front teeth flashed in his grin, I knew he was healthy and happy. I knew I had done it. I had created him and brought him into the world, and I knew I could do anything. I woke every day to my son babbling "puh puh puh", which meant "up up up", and I knew I'd make it through the day, the week, and many years to come.

Empowerment came as a surprise when I was just trying to survive. It wasn't granted to me; I suppose I earned it, but I would never have found it alone. It sprang up in the need to create a world for my son that was better than the one I had known before his arrival. Empowerment came with the growing connection to my son and a sense of fulfillment I had not known I was missing.

Mornings

❧

Rolling over and patting my pillow, I mumble, "You get up with him today." My lips, thick with sleep, resist movement. I open one eye slowly and blink to loosen my eyelashes, then struggle to read the red numbers of the clock. It shouts at me, "5:42."

I reach over and switch the small knob on the alarm, setting it to off. It's set for 6:10, just as it has been for nearly two years, but I don't remember what it sounds like. We never seem to make it long enough for the alarm to do its job.

"Mama, where are you?" My son's voice drifts up the stairs from his room to mine. He has been my alarm clock for the past twenty months. "Mama? Where are you?" His voice carries the essence of playgrounds, pony rides, and sand castles, flowers and dirt.

The empty pillow beside me is cool to the touch. I stare

at it a moment, wishing someone would be there, someone to answer my plea, to answer Dev's pleas, to get out of bed in the morning darkness, and to sacrifice their bare toes to the cold floor in my stead.

"Damn," I mumble into my pillow. It is easier when Dev wakes up crying because then I know he isn't done sleeping, and he'll drift off again in a matter of minutes. I hold my breath, and with it the hope that his pattern will change today. Let this be the day he just falls right back to sleep.

"Mama?" His voice dances up the stairs and skips across the floor. "Where are you?"

"I'm sleeping," I yell, pulling my pillow over my head.

A giggle is my answer. "Sheep fall down, Mama," he starts, conversationally, and I wonder why children don't come with programmable alarm clocks.

After fifteen minutes, and I don't know how many more calls of "Where are you?", I climb out of bed and pull fuzzy socks over my numb feet. As I start down the stairs, he laughs.

"Mama, coming," he says to the audience of assorted stuffed creatures we call his bedtime friends.

An infectious smile washes across his face as I appear at the foot of the stairs, and I can't help smiling in return.

He jumps up and down. The crib, which long ago held the infant version of my father, squeaks and groans in protest.

"Sheep fall down," Dev says, and he points to a small woolen sheep on the floor, his smile replaced by a look of genuine concern for a fallen comrade. "Pooh Bear sad."

"Oh, no," I croon sympathetically and pick up the soft

22

stuffed sheep that we bought on a trip to the Cotswold's, returning it to my son. I kiss Dev, the sheep, Pooh Bear, Willow Elf, Mr. Lion, and Titch the bear. Dev's smile returns.

"Milk, Mama?"

"Sure," I reply, scooping him from the crib. "Hug and squeeze," I say, and he wraps his arms and legs around me.

We pad through the chilly house, welded together with love made fresh by song birds and morning dew. Like most mornings, once the pain of pulling myself from my warm bed has passed, I'm selfishly pleased not to have to share this time of day. There's no one to come in with a booming voice and lure my boy away from me with promises of wild fun and male bonding.

Armed with a sippy-cup of milk and a few Nilla Wafers, I gather up clean clothes from a pile of hastily folded laundry, and we march to the bathroom. Dev settles himself on the floor next to the door with his milk, cookies, blanket, and toys. I manage to get my contacts into my swollen eyes after several false tries.

"Brush teeth, Mama," Dev whines, his hand stretched toward me, his fingers opening and closing.

I rinse off his toothbrush, getting it fully wet, and hand it to him. While I brush the taste of exhaustion from my mouth, he chews his dinosaur toothbrush, sucking the water off the bristles.

I start the shower and wait eagerly for the hot water to reach this end of the house. I pull at a hair on my leg to test its length. Peeking around the shower curtain, I'm pleased to see

Dev looking at a book, a soggy cookie held tightly in one hand. Perhaps I have time to shave.

"Mama?" Dev says, as I hear the book drop to the floor. "My shower."

"Not today." I return the razor to its home, unused. I try to remember the last time the razor had been used, but it's no use; it's been too long.

Quickly finishing, I try also to remember the last time I had a leisurely, private shower. I wonder, not for the first time, if there are babysitters for hire who will come into your house just for those times when you really need another pair of hands, another set of eyes, those times when you want to take a shower, go to the bathroom alone, cook dinner, watch the news, read a book, or do the laundry.

Hurrying through our morning, I pack up our gear for the day, make Dev his usual jelly toast, and pour myself a very large mug of coffee.

"Mama's bags, Dev's bag, blanket, milk." My son and I go through our daily checklist in unison. We pile into the car and head for his day care, which we call school.

"Dev's Mama," he sings from the back seat, the words pushing past the thumb that rarely leaves his mouth. "I love Mama."

I look in the baby-mirror clipped to the passenger side visor and smile at my son's reflection, glad again that this is all mine with no distractions or diversions, glad I don't have to share this moment either.

Routine Kisses

This essay was first published in Parenting New Hampshire *in 2000.*

CB

I've never been good at routines and rituals. Getting into the habit of a thing, over and over, time after time, has always been difficult for me. This makes taking vitamins, exercising, and getting to work on time difficult tasks to maintain. I pride myself in being "unpredictable." Routines are boring.

When I was pregnant, and reading all the parenting books I could find, I discovered that pediatricians highly recommend rituals and routines for children. The experts all explained that this gives a sense of security and control. For me, this was probably the most intimidating part of becoming a parent.

How am I going to set up routines and rituals for my child to follow when I can't do this myself? How will I ever survive the predictability and boredom of it?

As my son grows, I try to implement schedules and routines. The bedtime routine always falls short. Some nights we read, others we snuggle and talk. Some nights we remember to brush his teeth, and some nights he falls asleep in my lap. Some nights he gets into bed willingly, while others we have a full-blown battle. But he always goes to bed between 7:30 and 8:00. Therein lies the routine, I tell myself.

I tried rituals around bath time with equal inadequacy. I never know what days I'll be able to put him in the tub from one week to the next. He won't stand still for lotions or baby massage. One day he'll insist on washing, drying, and dressing himself, the next time he won't be willing to do any of it himself.

Then, one morning, it occurred to me that we had succeeded in setting up one routine, one set of rituals that we both counted on. Every morning, Monday through Friday, my son wakes me up by calling out "Mama, I'm awake." While I put in my contacts and brush my teeth, he chats, telling me about a dream he remembers or something that happened at day care. Then, I get him settled on the couch, his blanket tucked under him and another covering him. I turn on the Disney channel, fix a cup of milk, and get him a vitamin. I always tell him the flavor and shape of his vitamin as I give it to him (orange lions are his favorite). If he gets a cherry one he always reminds me that his cousin Michael does not like cherry. I hand him his milk in a spill proof cup and tuck the blanket around him again. I kiss his forehead several times, tell him I love him, and head for the shower.

I realize that for all my resistance to routine, one had

naturally evolved, enabling us to get up and out of the house every morning. We depend on it, thrive on it. It brings us closer together and allows us to move through the morning in harmony. Best of all, it's the only way I manage to shower in privacy. We move through the morning in fluid routine, and I try to never forget the kiss.

Dads for Sale

Originally published in Our Times, *January 2002, as "Understanding the Distinctions Between Fathers and Dads"*

My son has never known his father. We were divorced before Dev was born, and he has remained predominately absent ever since. Forever concerned with the impact this would have on my son, I've read numerous books and articles giving advice on how to explain an absentee parent to your child.

Fathers and dads are not the same thing. I took this advice to heart, and starting from a very young age, I have made this distinction for my son. Everyone has a father. Fathers are necessary to create children. The politically correct terminology we've all heard time and again is "biological father." A dad is a completely different beast, and not everyone has a dad. Dads, I explain to my son, help to care for their children, play with their children, and spend time with their children.

Many hours have been spent in my house discussing the different types of families. Always, the message is the same. Some families have a mom and a dad, some just have a mom, some just have a dad.

"You have a father," I assure my son. "He lives far away, and we don't see him. But, our family does not have a dad."

From time to time, especially as he has grown older, my explanations and assurances are met with questions. The questions get more pointed and insightful as we grow — and more difficult to answer. Each time, I conscientiously try to give my son a little more information, ever vigilant not to overload him, walking that fine line between enough and too much.

After a while, my son took a different tact. He stopped asking about his father and decided to adopt a dad. I became aware of this one day at the children's museum. As my brother and I chatted, my son wrapped himself around one of his uncle's legs. My nephew quickly wrapped himself around the other. It wasn't long before their voices raised over our own. They were staring intently at each other, yelling.

"He's my dad."

"No, he's my dad."

"No, he's my dad."

It was time for another discussion with my son. I explained that this was his uncle, and therefore not his dad. And, that as sorry as I was, our family does not have a dad. He assured me he understood and that he was fine. Then he announced to some acquaintances of mine that his grandfather was his dad. I not only had to explain the situation to my son again, but I had to explain it to others. Still, he insisted that his grandfather was his dad, and I had to trust that no one would actually believe him.

Every now and again, we have the discussion, we review the facts, and I feel temporarily appeased that he understands. Until one week came, when they discussed family at day care, and his classmates asked about his dad.

"I don't have a dad," Dev told them. "My mom hasn't bought me a dad or a sister yet. She's waiting for them to go on sale."

It was a year later, in pre-school, when the schedule announced they would be discussing family again. I held my breath, wondering where it would take us this time. I waited, asking every day about school, their projects and what was on his mind, but the issue never came up. A feeling of relief swept over me that I didn't quite trust. Was it possible that he was all set with the situation — at least for the time being? Was it possible that he accepted his family configuration, whether he understood it or not?

My answers came one afternoon when the teacher told me about their day. Dev had been sitting with several friends, making frames for pictures of their families. While the other children had nice snapshots of two parents with one or more children, Dev's picture contained just the two of us.

"Why don't you have a picture of your dad?" his friends asked.

"I don't have a dad," Dev said.

"What do you mean? How can you not have a dad?" they pressed.

"I have a father," Dev said. "Everyone has a father, but

my family doesn't have a dad."

"Oh," they said, taking in this new look at life.

"Is my dad also my father?" one friend asked.

"Probably," Dev explained. "If he lives with you then I think he's your father and your dad." He glued brightly colored pieces around the picture of us, his family. "I just have my mom," he continued, "and I'm fine with that."

Control Crackers

ॐ

There is almost nothing more frightening for a parent than thinking something might be wrong with your child, except for the nightmare of something actually being wrong. When Dev was very young, he tended to have streaks of aggression and complete loss of control. I don't mean the usual tantrums and fits that accompany the "terrible twos". This was far more, more aggressive and more angry than you'd think possible for a two-year-old, and I was concerned. Anyone who knows me knows I'm a worrier, justified or not, but this was different. My normally funny, sweet, and charming boy regularly appeared to be the spawn of Jekyll-and-Hyde.

When Dev was not quite two years old, we went on a family vacation to Disney World. With a large group of people, all having different tastes and agendas, it wasn't always easy to keep everyone on the same schedule for activities, eating, shopping, and sleeping. Not long into the trip, Dev's moods became erratic. He didn't like hanging around while others shopped; I agreed with him on that. But, he kept getting angry and impossible to calm or control. One day he was so agitated that he continuously tried to run away in the middle of Animal Kingdom. He was screaming at the top of his voice, throwing the mother of all temper tantrums. I picked him up, his back against me, and wrapped my arms around him, holding on for dear life while he kicked and punched and screamed. Finally, he let out a long wail, then closed his mouth on the top of my hand, biting down with all his might. I had a full set of teeth marks, upper and lower, on the top of my hand for a week.

Months went by with these episodes of outrage from my normally wild but good-humored boy. I found myself apologizing to his day care teachers on a regular basis, unable to explain why he would go into these spirals of anger and unable to help predict or prevent them. Some days I sat on the floor, holding him tightly in a full body lock, while he thrashed and screamed, and we both cried.

Though he was still very young, I consulted a child psychiatrist, more for peace of mind and coping strategies than for answers. Dev was quite verbal for his age, but obviously still too young to explain whatever was going on inside of him. The only thing the doctor could tell me was that Dev had a very healthy attachment to and trust in me and hopefully whatever was happening would work itself out as he got older.

We went through stretches when life seemed to click and

flow without incident, when we could settle into our own routine way of getting through day to day, and my son was happy, funny, cooperative, and sweet. These smooth stretches seemed mostly to fall on weekends, when we were together, and I worried that the angry outbursts were coming in protest to long days at day care while I was at work. There was nothing I could do about that; I had to work, but the pressure of guilt was taking a toll.

The episodes didn't just happen at day care. They seemed unpredictable. One minute all was well, and the next, he was completely out of control or in a full-on rage. I noticed that the problems occurred most often on the days when we were busy or when he was off with other people and not sticking to a schedule. This was also disconcerting because we did not exactly have the most regular, scheduled life, and I wanted, really needed, Dev to be adaptable and go with the flow.

One afternoon, when I picked Dev up at day care, his teacher pulled me aside. I knew immediately, by the look of concern on her face and the quiver in her voice, that whatever she had to say wasn't going to be good. Dev had been out of control, worse than ever. He had pounded with both fists on the large windows, screaming and beating the glass, and they couldn't get him to stop. They were afraid he'd break the window. The teacher had to pick him up, take him out of the recreation room, and wrap her arms tightly around him in a body lock.

His teachers had been making notes, and they realized that he began to lose control in mid-afternoon each day. It was like a switch being turned on, or perhaps turned off, between three and four o'clock each afternoon. I started keeping better track of Dev's beast-like episodes at home as well, and a pattern began to emerge. If Dev went more than three hours without eating, his mood changed. The longer he went between meals the greater the change in his personality. His Jekyll-and-Hyde transformations seemed to be driven by eating or, rather, not eating.

To test my theory, I enacted a new policy and insisted that Dev eat every two and a half to three hours, but never more than three hours between meals. I didn't worry about what it was, as long as he had something to eat. At day care, I asked that they give him something to eat mid-afternoon each day, though the kids did not normally get an afternoon snack. I brought in boxes of peanut butter and cheese crackers, which we quickly dubbed "control crackers". The adults in his life treated them more like a medication, though Dev just thought he was extra special because he got an afternoon snack.

Like magic, Dev's moods evened out, and the episodes of rage disappeared. His doctor confirmed a diagnosis of hypoglycemia, and a new world order began. Rule number one for anyone who spent time with Dev: have plenty of snacks on hand and feed him often. It was years until I ever left the house without at least a couple of packages of control crackers in my bag. We had control crackers in the car, at day care, in my coat pockets, in every room in the house, and in every bag we ever used.

Dev's eating habits became a bit unusual. He ate small

deconstructed meals throughout the day that were more like snacks. Instead of sitting down for a sandwich, chips, and grapes for lunch, he would eat half a sandwich, followed an hour later by the chips, and an hour later by the grapes, throughout the day. He became a grazer rather than a meal eater, but in the end, with control crackers always at the ready, everyone was happier for it.

The Gender Thing

Originally published in Our Times, *February 2002, as "Sitting Down on this Job Wasn't an Option"*

ℭℬ

It's easy to see how parenting in a traditional two-parent, two-gender family can have its advantages when gender issues start to creep out from behind the sofa. When I found out I was having a boy it occurred to me that issues would probably arise that I was not gender-trained to handle. I tried to prepare myself as best I could, but I wasn't sure exactly what would come up or when.

The first such situation took me a little by surprise when my son was two and a half and ready to potty-train. It occurred to me, for the first time, that I had no concept of how to pee standing up, or how to explain it to Dev. So, in the beginning, I encouraged him to sit, and he went along with that, not fully aware he had any other options. But, at day care he gradually realized that some of the other boys were doing it differently, and he just had to be like them.

I turned to the teachers, asking how they handled it. They were all women. How did they explain to the little boys the art of peeing while standing?

"We encourage them to sit," was the flat answer.

Sitting was quickly becoming less and less of an option, so we gave it a try. He tried standing. I tried helping and encouraging. We ended up with a big mess and a ton of laundry.

Finally, I turned to friends.

"How does your husband do it?" I asked. In turn, one of my friends actually asked her husband, reporting back the details.

"He'll probably need to use two hands," he warned. "At least to start, until he gets used to it. Make sure his feet are apart and his clothes are out of the way." The details went on, while I tried to visualize the process so I could help my son.

We had greater success, but we were still uncomfortable, unsure of what we were doing. And then the solution hit me – we went to my sister's house, and her husband spent the weekend helping Dev perfect this uniquely male talent.

It was during a discussion of this scenario, with a male friend of mine, that the question of boy's underwear came up. I knew no more about my son's little briefs than that they were cute. But, what of that mysterious flap in the front, where the fabric folds over and a gap is left like a secret passageway? What's that all about? I assumed it was for quick and ready access, facilitating the process of stand-up peeing. An aspect I had already resolved to ignore.

"God no," my friend gasped, horror on his face. "The

poor kid would hurt himself. The opening isn't big enough to do that sort of manipulation."

Images of my son going through some torturous acrobatics with his little-boy parts flashed through my mind, all because I had no clue about guy's underwear. The opening, my friend went on to explain, provides room to move and breathe, some give-and-take so nothing gets too cramped.

Having survived this ordeal, I took a deep breath and prayed the next issue wouldn't come up for awhile. Alas, it was not long before we entered into the-naming-of-the-parts phase. My son, suddenly aware that there were differences between boys and girls, wanted labels for these differences. He wanted to know what everything was called.

I was determined to give him these names in a matter-of-fact, no-nonsense, and truthful way. I wanted him to know the actual names and to have some respect. And so, quietly, subtly, I answered the questions as they came up, feeling rather secure in my approach and my success.

Then one day I woke up to my son, standing beside my bed, panic in his voice.

"Mama, Mama!"

I snapped my eyes open, instantly concerned.

"What is it? What happened?"

"Mama, your breasts are on the floor!" He pointed across the room to where my bra lay on the floor, hastily discarded the night before. He had the names and the respect, even concern, but he was still lacking some understanding.

I pulled him into my bed, wrapping my arms tightly

around him. Smiling, I reassured him that all was fine and everything was exactly where it was supposed to be.

A Tissue in Every Pocket

CB

A friend asked if I had a tissue with me, while we were out window shopping one day. Before I could look or reply, she said, "Of course, you must. All mothers have tissues." It was true that all mothers were in constant need of tissues, napkins, or wipes. But did we actually always have them on us?

I seemed to be in a perpetual state of looking for napkins and tissues. And, I'd become an expert on where to find them. While Dev was still quite young, I developed a specialized form of kleptomania – skillfully snatching napkins wherever I went with the stealth usually attributed to the world's superspies. The grocery store where we usually do our shopping has dispensers of folded white napkins around the meat coolers. Even when I'm not planning to buy meat, I meander by the coolers, and when I'm sure no one is nearby or paying attention, I pocket a handful, or two, of the thin napkins. The vendors in the food court at the mall keep dispensers of multi-colored, logo-adorned napkins out on the counters. Gas stations usually have those nice paper towels in hanging dispensers between the gas pumps; they're intended for cleaning the car windshield but work well on an assortment of spills and messes inside the car.

Whenever I found a ready source of napkins or tissues, I couldn't just take one or two, though I know that would be the normal, responsible approach. My compulsion demanded I take a healthy stack every time. Even if my son was remarkably free of goo at that particular moment, I helped myself to a few napkins at every opportunity that presented itself, stuffing them into a pocket or bag.

I wasn't always this way. Before Dev was born, I never had napkins or tissues on me. I was the one asking everyone else if they had a tissue to spare. If I happened to have a cold, I was known to grab a roll of toilet paper and carry that with me. It just never occurred to me to pick up an actual box of tissues.

Desperately curious if I had undergone this transformation that my friend seemed to imply came with motherhood—that somewhere along the way I would have squirreled away tissues and napkins—I decided to search my bags, pockets, and backpacks. It seemed to me that I was usually in search of them and never had them, so surely, I wouldn't have any stashed away. Any tissues and napkins I might have gathered along my way must have been used up with my son's recent allergy attack, I thought, or the chocolate chip granola bar

I gave him, or the cup of coffee I couldn't quite hold onto on the way to work.

I thought about the day I desperately needed an allergy pill and searched every pocket, nook, and cranny of my bags for just one bubble pack of that beautiful, pink and white Benadryl capsule. Instead, I found a treasure of hot wheel cars, Lego people, and crayons, a bag of animal crackers, a pack of cheese and peanut butter crackers crushed into a fine dust, and several sticky lollipops. Certainly, if something so critical as an allergy pill had been usurped by my son's possessions, how would it have been possible for tissues and napkins to gain a stronghold on any territory I maintained.

Unzipping my son's backpack, usually used for toys, I found a small stash of napkins with light blue daisies dancing across the quilted surface. In the large diaper bag we hadn't used for nearly a year, I found several brown Kraft-paper napkins, a container of dried-out wipes, and a small pile of neatly folded toilet paper. In my backpack, which doubled as our beach bag, was a thick pile of napkins with a wide assortment of logos and designs, perhaps gathered at the food court. There was also a small stash of stiff, balled-up napkins, which I quickly threw away. My pocket book had several well worn, but clean, tissues; as did my briefcase. My spring jackets and winter coat all had several napkins and tissues tucked neatly into each of their pockets. I knew, without checking, that the glove compartment and the arm-rest compartment in my car were both stuffed with napkins, paper towels, and tissues, and didn't bother retrieving them.

I looked at the small pile of paper in front of me and smiled. I didn't know if it was confirmation of my tissue-kleptomania or a deep seeded need to always be prepared that I had never been aware of. Perhaps it was true, perhaps my friend was right, I thought—perhaps mothers do have tissues in every pocket.

A Real Sports Mom

Originally published in Our Times, *February 2002, as "A Real Sports Mom Considers the Sidelines"*

CB

I have to admit, I'm jealous of the soccer moms and hockey moms I see loading up their cars and carting buckets of kids to practice and games. Juggling schedules and equipment, they get the kids to the field. But when it comes to the actual playing of the sports, they send the kids out in the yard with their husbands.

It's not that easy when you're the single mother of an active boy. As fate would have it, my son is a sports addict — it doesn't matter which sport. Since birth, his favorite toy has always been a ball. We have a collection that rivals what's available at MVP Sports, in every size, shape, and color imaginable.

Having older cousins has perpetuated this issue. He sees them playing hockey and soccer, and skateboarding, and he just has to do the same. By the time he was five, he had already tried soccer, ice skating, basketball, baseball, bicycling, roller blades, gymnastics, and more. I don't think he could choose just one if he had to.

I, on the other hand, have never been a sports fan. Growing up, I also tried just about every sport out there. But unlike Dev, the only one I enjoyed was soccer. I never had much interest in playing, or even watching, other sports. This poses a problem in my household. How do you find a middle ground between a mother with no interest in sports and a boy who wants to do nothing else?

When Dev wants to play baseball, I load up the car with bats, balls, and bug spray, and off to the field we go. When he wants to play soccer, we dig out the ball, add more bug spray, lace up the sneakers, and out in the yard we go. Unlike many other mothers, there is no one else around to go out with him, to play sports with him. Unlike most sports moms, whose involvement means doing the carpool and watching from the sidelines, this sports mom has to actually play the sport.

I push my sleeves up, pitch the ball, and endure the ridicule as the ball lands softly three feet in front of him.

"That's a bad throw, Mama," Dev scowls. "Don't joke. Play for real."

I'm too ashamed to tell him that I'm not joking and can't play baseball. I find myself apologizing repeatedly when I'm not able to show him the correct way to throw a football, dribble a basketball, or hold a hockey stick. I silently swear at the universe when my son begs me to explain the rules of a game on television or teach him how to box.

The whole situation has begun to rock my confidence. I've managed a successful consulting business for fifteen years and have written several books. I've found my way, alone, around foreign countries without wandering into harm's way. Yet I can't manage to keep up with my five-year-old sports fanatic.

Rubbing my sore muscles, after yet another one-on-one scrimmage, I wonder if there's another way. I toy with the idea of saying no the next time he asks to play baseball, football, or basketball. For a moment, I'm relieved when I think about the day that will come, when he's old enough to play on a team and have a coach. The day when I will no longer have to risk injury and humiliation in the name of sports. It's then that I remember why I always say yes — to give my son what he needs most. To give him the things that most boys have, and to get as close as I can to a normal life without a dad in the family. And suddenly I'm saddened by the thought that he will soon have teams and coaches, and I will be like the other sports moms — watching from the sidelines.

Getting it All Done

Originally published in Our Times, *April 2002,*

❧

Like most women over thirty, and probably many younger, I've always believed that I had to do it all and take care of everything. The house should be in order, dinner should be home cooked, and the laundry should be cleaned and neatly folded. As a single mother, I felt an extra drive to prove that I could handle it all without skipping a beat. It's amazing how quickly you learn to do things with one hand, balancing a baby on the opposite hip. I don't remember the last time I simply walked from one room to another without accomplishing something in the process, returning toys to my son's room, dirty dishes to the kitchen, and paper to the trash.

A friend of mine frequently told me, "Just because you can, doesn't mean you have to do it all yourself."

At times I'd want to snap at her, "I can take care of it myself." I was self-sufficient, and I wanted to be sure everyone understood that. But at other times I was relieved when she'd step in and help me out. Just to be able to hold my son with both hands was somewhat of a luxury.

People have always asked how I manage on my own. I smile, and say, "You have to accept that not everything gets done." Secretly, I hope this will explain why the house is a mess and my whites aren't really white. But a knot always forms in my stomach, and I rush home to do the dishes or the vacuuming.

For a long time I struggled with my schedule, certain that if I planned my time correctly I could fit it all in. I would print blank monthly calendars from my computer and try to plan my time more efficiently. I blocked in time for writing, taking care of Dev, doing the laundry, visiting family, and cleaning. I would look at the carefully thought out schedule and nod to myself, reassured that I could do it all.

But weeks later I would find the calendars in a stack of unread newspapers and unopened bills and realize that I hadn't found time for cleaning or laundry in weeks. I'd put the papers with Dev's coloring supplies and try to make a dent in the pile of dirty clothes.

Week after week something would get missed. From one phone call to the next, I conveyed my apologies for not returning a call, for not meeting a commitment. I compiled lists of upcoming birthdays and anniversaries, including those I'd forgotten from the previous month, sneezing as I noticed the depth of dust on the table.

It finally occurred to me one night, as I brushed crumbs

from the bottom of my feet before getting into bed, that I wasn't keeping up—I really couldn't do it all by myself. I cried at that realization.

I wasn't prepared to sacrifice the narrow window of time I manage to etch out for Dev, and I can't afford to stop working. I scoured the schedule looking for what to cut and where to shave off time. As it was, I had no personal time scheduled and none to give up. There was only one answer— the cleaning had to go.

Despite fears of a stranger rummaging through my house, knowing my darkest secrets and failures, and finding the layers of grime undisturbed for months, I called a cleaning service. I remember opening the door nervously, the first day the cleaning person had been scheduled. The aromas of lemon and pine slapped me in the face. The kitchen counter sparkled. I thought I had wandered into heaven.

These days, when people ask me how I manage it by myself, I continue to answer, "You have to accept that not everything gets done." But I am no longer hiding behind this answer, afraid of being found out. I freely accept that I can't do it all and strive to do only what matters most. The plants have all died off, toys are usually scattered from one end of the house to the other, and there is always a mountain of laundry waiting.

The important things are always taken care of. There's time to play games with Dev and read him stories. We have good food in the fridge and a bag full of well-worn sports equipment in the garage. On cleaning days, I slip my shoes off and walk across the spotless floor. Looking at the crumb-free soles of my feet, I smile. My illusions of being super woman are indeed dead, but I don't care, my son is happy, and my floor feels great under my bare feet.

Manipulating Adults

Originally published in Our Times, *May 2002,*

CƷ

Most people can remember manipulating their parents and playing them against each other to get what they want. All kids seem to instinctually know the art of moving from one parent to the other until they find satisfaction. If Mom says no, just go ask Dad. If Dad says no, try Mom again. Kids learn to identify what each parent is most likely to say yes to. They celebrate their good fortune when the response is "go ask your mother" or "go ask your father".

Maybe it's a deep seeded control issue, but I've always been quite happy that this was one childhood trick I wouldn't have to deal with from my son. If I say no then that's that. There is no one else to turn to, no one else to get a yes from. I get to set the rules, without being side-stepped, second-guessed, undermined, or over-ruled. Or so I thought.

But nature perseveres, and, as is every child's birthright,

my son has found a way to get around me. Despite my efforts, he manages to find adults to play against me and get what he wants. In a way, it's like he saves up all the no's I give him and keeps a running tally. The things he suspects I'll say no to seem to go at the top of the list, and he doesn't even bother asking me. Then, as soon as he is in the care of another adult, he reviews the list. Instinct kicks in, and he goes for the gold.

"Mom said I can have soda today," he tells the babysitter over lunch. "She said I can because I ate all my breakfast."

Unfortunately for Dev, the babysitter is fully aware of my strict no-soda policy. She deftly avoids his trap, maneuvering around his tactics, keeping one rule in place.

"Can I have some chocolate," he asks his aunt, moments after I leave for the store.

"Did your Mom say you can?" my sister always asks, despite my warnings that it's never a good idea to take a five-year-old at his word.

Dev assures her that I had said yes—as though it was a simple oversight on my part to leave the house without giving him the chocolate in the first place—when in fact I had expressly told him no chocolate shortly before my sister's arrival. Upon my return, it takes him about five minutes to confess that his aunt let him have the chocolate even though I had said no, like it had been her idea all along and she had practically forced it on him.

Despite not being able to make use of this particular kid-skill on a daily basis, Dev has still managed to put it to good use, and not just to get sugar.

"Mommy doesn't let me watch this movie," he tells my sister, holding up a video. "But since she's not home I think it's okay."

This time my sister doesn't buy into his attempt, and the movie is vetoed. But he has managed to see a number of shows and movies that had been previously prohibited by my feeble "no." He delights in telling me that he gets to watch the *Butt Ugly Martians* at his uncle's house, knowing that the show's name alone makes me want to bring the TV to the dump. The rules over there are different, and I'm outranked.

He pulls out all his tricks when my parents are around, going straight to the source he knows will satisfy. One afternoon Dev went off with my father to run errands. I gently reminded them that a nutritional lunch would be in order, though I didn't hold much hope for that happening. When they arrived back home Dev was carrying a slushy and a bag of licorice. He had several new toys, including a new football, and grass stained knees. Instead of errands they went toy shopping and then to the park. When pressed regarding lunch, the response was simple.

"I thought about tacos, chicken nuggets, and French fries, Mom," Dev responded. "But all I wanted was the slushy."

I've tried taking a different tack, explaining that our rules still apply, even when he's not home. But I know that lecture has even less power then the original verdict of no.

The flaw in my son's instinctual quest to get away with

the forbidden is his impulsive need to confess. He always tells me when he gets away with something, and it rarely takes him ten minutes to come clean.

"I'm sorry, Mama, but," he always starts, followed by the list of infringements he managed to finagle from his aunt, uncle, or grandparents in my absence.

On a number of occasions, I have toyed with the idea of typing up a set of instructions to go along with him, listing the rules that I have decided to enforce. No sugar or soda, no violent toys or movies, no *Sponge Bob, Simpsons,* or *Cat Dog.* And no *Butt Ugly Martians*! But then I think about it and realize that this would be depriving my son of his natural right to try and get away with whatever he can, using any means at his disposal. And who am I to deprive my son of the opportunity to manipulate the grown-ups in his life. I realize that it's my job to try and set the rules, but it's his job to try and break the rules any way he can.

The Meaning of Father

Originally published in Our Times, *June 2002,*

CƷ

Every year, as summer roles in, the yard erupts in a symphony of color, and the neighborhood comes alive with the laughter of children. We look forward to exploring tide-pools, playing baseball, riding bikes, and rollerblading. We start planning our summer camping trips and visits with family and friends. But before we can get to all this fun, we have to get past Father's Day.

It starts early, with the commercials and preparations, on television and at school. At home, it starts with a subtle change in Dev's behavior. He becomes edgier, pushing his boundaries, sucking his thumb and whining more often. It's so subtle, in fact, that I almost don't recognize it. But then I remember, June is approaching and with it comes Father's Day. As the day grows closer, and more publicized, my son's behavior gets scarier. It takes a couple of weeks before he is ready to talk about what's going on. The approach of Father's Day rais-es questions about his own absentee father. It is a glaring annual reminder of what he is missing.

Year after year, I discuss the pending holiday with his teachers and come up with a plan to make the event pass easier for him. Dev and I discuss, again, what makes a family and the difference between fathers and dads, and I strive to help him understand and accept his situation. Each year, when his class sits down to make their Father's Day gifts, Dev chooses which of the men in his life will be the happy recipient of his hand-crafted affections. He proudly bestows rice crispy treats, hand prints, and paintings on his grandfather and uncle, bravely wishing them a happy Father's Day.

I decided to take a new tact. After all, we can't deny that the world is full of fathers, and my son is too aware to ignore that we don't have one in our family. I started a discussion with him on what it means to be a good father. We talk about different kinds of fathers, the things that make fathers special and all the things that good fathers do with their children and for their families. We talk about the kind of father we would like to have in our family. We look at all the men that mean so much to us—my father, brother, and brothers-in-law, friends, and honorary uncles. What we have decided, my son and I, is that there are many things that make a father special, whether they live with their children or not.

Fathers wrestle with you and willingly allow you to pin them to the ground. They play sports with you, teach you to throw a football and hit a baseball. Fathers protect you when there's a lightening storm and give you ice cream for breakfast. They buy you real tools and teach you to build, make up stories and bring you to watch airplanes. They don't mind getting dirty, touching bugs, and walking in seaweed. Fathers know when you need juice, peanut butter sandwiches, or tickles. They get excited when you make it to the next level of a video game and don't tell you to calm down every time you want to play ninja warrior. Fathers will sit for hours-on-end building with Legos and racing Hot Wheels. They don't care if your shirt is untucked, if there are holes in the knees of your jeans, or if you go outside without your coat. They know all of the things you don't like, what you are afraid of, and what makes you nervous. They also know your favorite color, food, game, and book.

What makes a father special is that they spend time with their children, take care of their children, and love their children unconditionally. What makes them special is that they are there, day in and day out, week in and week out, sharing in their children's lives. Whether a father lives in the same home or not, whether a father talks to his children every day or only weekly, fathers are a very big part of every child's life. Even an absentee father plays a big part in his child's well-being. Fathers are one-half of what makes the child—physically and emotionally.

The number of single-fathers in the U.S. has been rising steadily over the past decades. According to the U.S. Census Families and Living Arrangements report, in the year 2000 there were over 2 million single-father families in the United

States; 5% of American families were single-father households, up from 1% in 1970. Like single-mothers, single-fathers have particular challenges that other fathers need not learn to deal with. As such, single-fathers deserve special recognition on Father's Day.

So, in honor of all the fathers out there who know their children, who put in the work and survive the inconvenience, who take care of their children with partners or alone, who love their children unconditionally, and who recognize the gifts they have been given in the little people who worship them — we wish you Happy Father's Day.

A Deep Connection

Originally published in Our Times, *July 2002,*

ᘓ

There's an interesting dynamic that forms between a child and a single parent. The child is privy to many of the parent's emotions, issues, and struggles. The roles of parent and friend become blurred. The child can become a confidante and sounding board, while chinks form in the parent's armor of strength.

Being single, there is not the daily opportunity to give voice to life's issues with another adult. There are no shoulders to cry on when the kids are asleep, no one immediately available to vent to after an argument with the boss. As a single mother, my choices are often limited—keep it all to myself or open up to my son. I learned early on that keeping my daily concerns locked up had a negative impact on both of us. I was stressed out, and Dev didn't know it wasn't about him.

After a particularly bad day at work that culminated in a blow-out argument with a manager, I was visibly upset. I knew my tension showed, and I knew that Dev sensed it. I was near tears for the entire ride home, and my voice was shaky.

"Are you sad, Mama?" Dev asked before we reached home. "Are you sad with me?"

That's when it struck me, like lightning. If I was going to carry my emotions around, just under the surface, with nowhere to vent, it was going to impact Dev.

Of course, the cares and concerns of the adult world are far too heavy for pre-school shoulders. Deciding when to let him in and when to find other ways to vent is difficult.

"I had a bad day at work," I finally answered. I weighed the words, trying to choose what to share and what to hold on to. "I had a fight with someone at work."

Dev was outraged. "Was he mean to you? Did he call you names?" His questions flew around the car.

"Yes," I admitted. "Someone was mean to me and called me names." I didn't tell him what the fight was about, the choice words that were hurled at me, that I felt I could no longer stand my job, or that I had no idea what to do about it. I tried to keep my admission to terms I was sure he could process.

"That big bully!" My son, confidante, and defender, raised his fist, shaking it in the air. "I won't let him be mean to you again."

From then on, when I would have a rough day at work or yet another argument with the manager, Dev would hug me.

"Was that big bully mean to you again?" he would ask, his voice full of concern.

I'd say yes, and he would echo back all of the strategies and suggestions I've given him for dealing with the bullies in his own life. And the world would be right again. My troubles vented, my spirits lifted, and the bully an ancient glitch in the day. But more than that, I would feel the bond strengthen between Dev and me.

There are many times when I know it is not appropriate to share my thoughts, concerns, and issues with Dev. I don't tell him when I start to panic over financial issues, or vent my frustrations regarding his father, or let him in on the depth of loneliness that can come with being a single-parent. These issues, which are far too heavy for a boy to carry, wait until I am able to connect with another adult, after Dev is in bed or while he's in school.

Without another adult in the house to draw my attention, I talk to Dev about my writing and art, sharing my excitement with him. I explain my goals and hopes to him, and involve him in some of my decisions. Together we plan wild African safaris, decide what color to paint the hallway, talk about events in our lives and the world, and daydream about having a bigger family someday.

Dev practices his writing and helps me organize my art supplies. When we have visitors he overflows with pride, giving tours of my office and studio space, as though my work zone was a new set of Legos. When my writing projects take us on the road, which happens frequently, he enthusiastically tags along, helping me spot sights and entertaining me in the car—all the while sharing his thoughts, feelings, and dreams, just as I have done with him.

Whenever it is realistic, I involve Dev in making decisions that impact our little family. He helps decide what we'll be having for dinner, what we'll be doing on the weekend, and what we'll do when on vacation. He helps with household chores—to the best of his ability—and joins me each year in planting new flowers in the garden. He has a stake in maintaining our family, which not only makes him a more willing player, but seems to give him an amazing sense of confidence.

We are connected in a unique way, each personally vested in the other's life. We lean on each other, regardless of what else is going on in the world around us. I share my life with Dev, letting him in on my emotions, dreams, and struggles. And in return he freely shares his life with me.

Avoiding Single Parent Burnout

Originally published in Our Times, *August 2002,*

ℭℬ

Life as a single parent can be challenging and exhausting. The stresses can easily build and take over. Burn-out is a real danger. There are a number of techniques and tools that I've found to be lifesavers, and that all single parents can use to make life easier and happier.

Plan and Prepare Ahead of Time - Each night, plan out the next day. Make lists of what must be accomplished. Pack the backpacks, book bags, and briefcases. Set out everything needed for school and work. Each Sunday, plan out the week, and make sure that everyone's schedules are in order. Planning ahead will ensure that everything gets done and significantly decrease the stress and pressure of running around at the last minute.

Rituals Make Life Move Smoother - Kids love rituals and routines, and they respond very well to them. A set bed time, with a bed time ritual, will help to make a happy end to the day. A predictable morning ritual may also help make it possible to shower in private. It's easier for everyone when they know what to expect and look forward to.

Save Special Time for Your Child - Be sure to schedule in special family time. Family game night is great for kids of all ages, as is story time, and pizza night. It's these good times that everyone will remember, and the anticipation of these events will keep everyone going through the week. Another idea is to come up with extra holidays and days of celebration that are specific to your child and your family. Celebrate half birthdays, adoption days, and the beginning of your favorite season.

Make the Most of Sick Days - It has been said that illness is nature's way of getting you to slow down. Spend sick days snuggling with your child, reading books, playing games, and enjoying each other. Caring for a sick child also strengthens the bond between you. Look at it as a gift rather than an inconvenience.

Spend Smartly So You Don't Have to Stress - Know the difference between what you need and what you want, and help your children to understand this difference as well. Watch your spending to the best of your ability. Money stresses can be one of the most powerful we have to face. Reduce that stress by being proactive and spending smartly.

Simplify Cooking - There are so many fabulous short cuts in the market now. Packages of pre-cut, pre-washed fresh vegetables, meats cut to size and marinated, packaged sauces that are delicious on pasta and pizza. Take advantage of these products for healthy and quick meals. When you do have time to cook, cook in bulk. Make enough for several meals and consider freezing portions. Make leftover night a habit—you don't have to cook, you don't have to waste food, and everyone gets to eat something different.

Just Do Your Best and Don't Compensate - Do your best, day in and day out, and be confident in that. Accept that you are doing the best you can. Don't waste time or energy feeling guilty or holding onto regrets. And don't make compensations that end up making life more difficult. If you are busy, don't compensate by letting your kids stay up too late, as it will only make it harder to get them to bed the next night.

Never Go To Bed Angry - Anger is another energy zapper, for both you and your child. End your child's day on a happy note so that everyone rests easily and you can enjoy your evening. Go in, when your child is dozing off, and give them an extra hug and kiss to ensure they know you are no longer angry.

Don't Take Anything Personally - Children have little control over what they say. It's common for children to say hurtful things when they are upset, even to the person most important to them. Also, there will be many people who will question, even criticize, what you do and how you do it. Don't take what they say personally.

Beware of Your Pet-peeves - We all have them. Those little things that set us off. Whining, dawdling, messy rooms, bad language, picky eating, whatever it may be. Acknowledge that this is your weakness, explain to your child that this is the one thing that really makes you angry, and work hard to control your moods.

Keep the Kids Informed - This is like the "honesty is the best policy" rule. No one likes unexpected disruptions in their routines and schedules, and children are particularly sensitive to changes. Let your child know what's going on, what to expect, and what not to expect. The more the child understands, the easier it is for him/her to go along with the family.

It takes work to keep everything moving along without incident, and it's not always possible. Simplifying your life and communicating with your children will help to smooth the way.

Sole Provider

Originally published in Our Times, *September 2002,, titled "More Than Financial Security"*

CB

It's natural instinct. As parents, we provide for our children. We are willing to do whatever we have to, to ensure the health, safety, and happiness of our offspring. We don't question it. We rarely even think about it.

I have been so busy providing for my little family that the days have started to run together and blur. I was barely aware of what day it was, when my son climbed into my bed one Saturday morning. He snuggled up beside me, as he always does, his beloved blanket falling across my face. It wasn't long before we broke into our customary tickle match, laughter shattering the morning peace.

All of a sudden, Dev stopped wiggling and tickling. He sat still, with his back straight, his face looking serious. "Mom," he said, quietly. "Can this be your day off?"

My heart nearly broke in half with the weight of the

guilt that those simple words generated.

"It's not fair," he continued, his sweet face somber and determined. "You work every day."

He was right, of course. In my determination to support and provide, I have fallen into a pattern of working every day. I didn't have the heart to tell him that that Saturday would be no different. I hesitated, then offered a compromise to do work that would require the least amount of concentration and time.

It isn't just a need to pay the mortgage or buy school clothes and groceries. There is also the fact that I'm self-employed, which seems to complicate things. I had decided, a while ago, that I should be able to provide for my family while doing work that I love to do. This has led to three fledgling businesses, which keep me working all day, everyday.

Financial pressures are arguably the biggest stressors we face, regardless of the number of providers in the family. Most of us live from check to check, avoiding the bill collectors, clipping coupons, and finding creative ways to make ends meet. As a single parent, the term sole provider takes on a very literal meaning. There is no choice in the matter. There is no one else to review the books with or decide who will work overtime, who will take on a second job, or who will move on to a new job. There is no one to co-sign loans or use their credit when yours is too scary. Every financial decision, and every debt, is your responsibility, alone.

However, that Saturday, as I looked into my son's face, which seemed serious and wise beyond his five years, it occurred to me—I am not just the sole financial provider for my family, I'm the sole everything provider. It's so easy to let the practical and financial aspects of life take over our lives and overwhelm us. But there is so much more providing that needs to be done.

As the sole-provider, I am the only one available to dispense Tylenol, kisses, and tickles. At night, I'm the only one to cover him when he's cold or calm him after a bad dream. I'm the only one that can make sure there is clean underwear each morning and pajamas at the end of the day. I am the teacher of riding bicycles, using chopsticks, boogie boarding, and catching crabs without getting pinched. My long list of responsibilities starts with supplying milk and vitamins in the morning and finding just the right cartoon, and doesn't end.

As parents we are responsible for every aspect of our child's health and welfare. As a single parent, I am solely responsible for every aspect of my child's health and welfare— from tickles and raspberries, to Lego skyscrapers and summer fun, to grilled cheese sandwiches. I struggle to keep my schedule in balance, keeping up with my work and our play. Whenever possible I include Dev in my work life and open myself up to his imaginary life. But most importantly, I try to take a day off and provide some fun for my family.

First Day of School

Originally published in Our Times, *October 2002,*

ℭℬ

Fall is a special time of year for Dev and me. The cool air brings a calmness with it that soothes and comforts us. We look forward to the eruption of color that sweeps through our neighborhood, checking our own trees each morning to monitor their progress and anxiously waiting for our burning bush to ignite with brightly colored leaves.

Over the past six years, Dev and I have developed a number of traditions that we look forward to as fall approaches - activities that help us wind down from a busy summer.

Each year we go to a harvest festival, picking apples and riding on wagons full of hay. We wander the pumpkin patch and trod over dried, spent corn stalks. We can't help sampling apples as we wade through the thick grass of the orchard in search of the perfect fruit, and top the day off with grilled corn-on-the-cob.

We also make it a point to trek out to Fryeburg, Maine, for the annual Fryeburg Fair. We spend the day on carnival rides, petting baby animals, and dodging the giant ones, all the while eating junk food. At the end of the day, before heading home, we drive along the Kancamagus Highway in search of early snow.

Our autumn usually culminates with an annual Halloween bash that we host for friends and family, complete with creepy games and way too much Halloween themed food.

This year we started a new tradition. One that will greet us at the end of summer, each year, for the next twelve, or more, years. This year we started school - real school.

The first day of Kindergarten brought with it an assortment of emotions, for both my son and me. After having him home with me all summer, we were both more than ready for school to begin. He was ready to be back into a routine, busy with friends and activities, learning and exploring. I was ready for my space, for peace and quiet, and the chance to get some writing done.

As the day approached, we both became more anxious. Excited for the new road in our lives to begin and nervous about the changes that lay ahead. This was my baby. My first. My one and only. Was it really possible that he could be old enough for real school?

During the final week of summer, we busied ourselves buying school supplies and trying on new clothes, preparing and planning. The anxiety was still there, but we managed to keep it at bay.

In the middle of all the preparation, as if I needed yet another reminder that my son was rapidly growing up, Dev lost his first tooth. He flashed his new grin, poking his tongue through the gaping hole where the tooth once stood. He called everyone we know, boasting of his missing tooth and new school supplies, the pride visible on his face.

We were ready for school. But what I wasn't ready for was having him transform from a five-year-old to a teenager before my eyes. It wasn't just that he looked so much older, dressed in his school clothes, with his knapsack on his back. It wasn't just in the proud swagger as he crossed the parking lot toward his new school, or that he actually, suddenly had a swagger. It was in the way he raised his palm, not waving to me but dismissing me, when I asked for hug.

"Bye, Mom," he said quickly. "Have a good day."

"Should I walk you to your class?" I asked, practically begging for him to toss me a morsel.

He looked at me as if I was an insane stranger. "No," he snapped. "I can do it myself."

The next day was worse. He didn't even take the time to look at me or dismiss me with his hand. He mumbled goodbye, his back already turned toward me, and off he marched.

That was that - he was done with me. My heart broke.

For a moment, I envied my fellow kindergarten parents who have smaller children still completely dependent. I envied those with older children, who have already learned, first hand, that this phase will pass as their children become confidant in their own independence. I envied those whose five-year-olds have not yet thrust them aside. And I envied those that have someone else at home to hug them when their kindergartener won't.

I looked around the parking lot, eyeing the other parents who lingered, watching the door that their child had disappeared behind. Most seemed to wear their resolve in their stiffened spines and half smiles - an odd combination of pride and distress. Single, married, or divorced, with co-parents or without, with multiple children or one, we were all in the same situation. In this, I knew I was not alone. We had all brought our off-spring to the edge of the nest, and like it or not, they were ready to try out their wings.

Sleeping Tight

Originally published in Our Times, *November 2002,*

CB

If a surgically implanted tracking device was available, would you want one for your child? That was the question a morning radio personality posed to his listeners one day, not long after I dropped my son off at school. I don't think the question had fully registered, but I was already answering yes.

Would I have my son wired, so that I could always know where he was? You bet.

As I drove, I thought about the implications more deeply. There is privacy, trust, and independence to consider, but a five-year-old has very little of these. In this uncertain life, the idea of being able to locate my son with the flip of a switch might be far too tempting to pass up. Assuming there were no health risks and no pain involved, I would probably not hesitate to have my son tracked — at least until he was a teenager, when privacy, trust, and independence become a much bigger deal.

The news is regularly filled with reports of children being taken from their homes, schools, and playgrounds. Boys and girls, from infants to teenagers, are all at risk. We set up passwords with our children and play "what if" games, instead of "I Spy", to teach them and keep them safe. Keeping our children out of harm's way, especially in a world that seems to grow more insane each day, is paramount for all parents.

The sense of urgency over the security of our children has not only infected us as parents but has begun to infect our children as well. A friend of mine recently told me that her ten-year-old has taken to locking all the downstairs windows before going to bed. He once enjoyed staying up by himself, watching TV and hanging out, after the rest of the family had gone upstairs. However, with all that has been going on in the world, he no longer stays downstairs by himself.

Dev has become hyper-conscious about being left alone or getting lost. If I leave him in the car, while I run into the house for something forgotten, he quickly locks his car door. If he ends up in the yard by himself, usually because the adults in his life can't keep up with him, he gets anxious.

"I can't be outside alone," he says. "You can't let me be alone because someone might steal me."

I cringe, and my heart aches. I long to give my son the carefree days of running around the neighborhood that I remember from my own childhood. I would love for him to experience a world where his biggest concern is to not squish the worms he catches, and where, as a child, the idea of getting stolen would never have crossed his mind.

Every night, as I tuck Dev into his bed, he says, "Don't forget to set the alarm, Mama." His voice sounds old and young at the same time. "Set it now, so we'll be safe."

"We're totally safe," I assure him, kissing his forehead.

"But what if a bad guy gets in?" he asks, wiggling down into his bed, his voice already fading.

"No one can get in," I promise him. "I won't let anyone get in."

I know what is next on his mind, even if he doesn't say it. He has said it enough on other nights. The question is out there, in his head and in our lives. How can I keep us secure? How can I protect us? Without a dad in the house, how can I ensure our safety?

"Bad guys are stronger than you," Dev has told me, more times than I care to remember. "How can you stop them? They are stronger and meaner than you, and they cheat."

He is right, in a way. Being home alone, with a five-year-old and two cats, doesn't always give me a strong and secure feeling either. But there is the security alarm. And fortunately, I don't tend toward panic or paranoia.

I make sure the basement door is locked and the windows to the deck are closed. I set the security alarm, check on Dev, say a prayer, and sleep soundly with the knowledge that we are secure and safe — even without a dad in the house — and that we are together, happy, and healthy.

Sibling Envy

Originally published in Our Times, *December 2002,*

ᘓ

It's the age-old dilemma. We want to fill our children's lives with happiness and make all of their dreams come true. We would love to give them everything they've ever wanted - without spoiling them, of course. It's hard to say no, but it's not always possible, or practical, to succumb to all of their whims.

Sometimes, we luck out and accept that grandparents or aunts can fulfill a desire we've put off or denied - like buying that special toy or allowing your child to eat popcorn for dinner.

Unfortunately, there are other times when as much as we may want to give in to our children's requests, we just can't, and neither can anyone else. Sometimes their desires and dreams are simply too big.

My son's dearest wish right now is for something that I, especially as a single parent, can't reasonably or realistically provide.

Dev is suffering from sibling envy. He is craving a little brother or sister as if it was an addiction. To be exact, as he has explained in detail on several occasions, he wants two little brothers and then a little sister.

This burning desire of his, to be a big brother, has shown itself in a number of ways. It's on his face and in his voice when he tries on the role with his younger cousins. He puts his arm around a toddler cousin, gently guiding her away from the dangerous stairs, and rushes to her rescue when she drops her sippy cup.

He has a list of people he would like to have as his big brothers, assuring me that a big brother would be almost as good as a little brother. His list includes Danny Zuko from *Grease*, the singer Aaron Carter, and our friend Joe. He also has a list of names he wants for his siblings - Danny, Aaron, and Jennifer.

"I think you should adopt a baby brother for me," Dev informed me one day.

"It's not that easy," I tried to tell him.

"Just adopt a brother for me," he said, as though it was a simple matter of running over to Walmart or Toys-R-Us. "We need a baby brother."

I can't argue with him. I wouldn't mind adding a baby brother to our family either. It doesn't help that I already feel he's missing out on so much with no father in the family - he shouldn't have to miss out on siblings as well. I try pointing out how busy we are and how much work I already have. I try telling him that we couldn't do all the things we love to do if we had a baby to take care of. He accepts my explanations, although I know he doesn't believe them any more than I do.

He assured me one day that he would be ready if I were to have a baby. "I know what to do if you're going to have a baby," Dev said.

A number of images flashed through my mind, in horror. What could he know? How could he know it? What kind of conversation was this to be having with a five-year-old boy?

"What would you do?" I asked tentatively and braced myself for the answer.

"You will get in the tub," he said, matter-of-factly. "And I will call nine-one-one. And then they'll come and take the baby out."

Words failed me. Finally, I assured him that this was not something we would have to worry about, since I was not planning to have a baby.

When we go to the playground, Dev pretends to be a big brother, finding a younger child to "adopt" on his own. He picks out a toddler, leading her around the playground. He shows her how to use all of the equipment, holding her hand at the tricky parts, gently warning her away from the dangerous parts, and tying her shoe laces whenever needed.

I watch with amazement. He would make a great big brother. I pray he doesn't think to ask Santa for a sibling, but, at the same time, I long to give him the little brother or sister he wants so badly. Or maybe a puppy will do.

Single Parent Families—Through the Eyes of Child

Originally published in Our Times, *January 2003*

CB

Every month, I write about my experiences as a single parent. Hopefully I hit on issues that all parents, single or not, are able to relate to. But, it occurred to me that I am usually looking at life from my single-parent's eyes. As I tried to decide what to write about this month, I began to wonder what Dev would have to say on the subject. The children are, after all, the most important piece of this puzzle. They are what keep us going and make it all worth while.

So, I sat down with Dev and asked him if he'd help me write my column for the newspaper. At first, he thought I was talking about one of my other writing projects and began making up stories about police officers. That was entertaining, but beside the point.

"Would you help me write the piece about us, for the newspaper?" I asked. "I'll ask you some questions, and I'll type in your answers."

"Sure," Dev said. He climbed up on the sofa beside me, crossed his legs, and gave me his full attention.

"What is a single parent?" I asked.

"Just one parent in the house," he answered, confidently.

"Do you know any single parents?"

Shaking his head side to side, he said, "No."

"What do you think it's like for people in single parent families?"

"Really hard work and really sad kids." He looked down, and his lips sagged.

"Why would the kids be sad?" I asked, quickly.

"Because they miss their dad or mom."

"What if they don't know their dad or mom?"

He looked at me, nodding his head and seemed to be deep in thought. "They should go to a dot-com and find their name to see what they can know," he said, finally, nodding again.

"What else do you think about families with single parents?" I asked.

"I think they should use a grandpa or grandma or uncle or aunt to have a mom or a dad."

"You mean, if they're missing their dad then they should use a grandpa or uncle?"

"Yeah."

I knew he was drawing this from his own personal experience. "For what kinds of things?" I asked.

"You know, to like take care of them. And if they don't have to work then they can take them to places that they really want to go, even if the mom says no."

More personal experience, I assumed.

"Do you think our family is a single parent family?"

"Yes, I do," he said, then paused. "No, I don't. I don't."

"Why not?" I was beginning to worry that somehow he really didn't understand our situation at all.

"Because they all have moms and dads," he said.

I realized then that he was thinking of our whole, large, extended family. "But I mean our family," I said. "You and me. Do you think our family is a single parent family?"

He looked up at me, his eyes large and face somber. "Yes, I do."

"How do you feel about that?"

"I feel a little sad and a little not."

"What parts make you sad?"

"That I can never see my father and that… I think that's the only thing… I don't know." He looked away, fidgeting.

"What parts are not sad?" I asked, quickly.

"The parts that I have you." He paused. "I think that's it."

"What do you like about having me?" I asked.

"That you feed me and love me and care about me… and you love me… and you take care of me." He leaned over and snuggled up against my arm.

"Yeah?" I asked, not wanting to move on from this suddenly tender moment.

84

"Umm hmmm. That's it."

"What are some of the hardest things about having just you and me in our family?"

Dev seemed to think for a while. "The hardest part," he started. "Hmmm. Let's see. Trying to take care of you like you take care of me. Trying to help you if you're sad or lonely. I think that's it."

"What are the best things about having just you and me in our family?"

"Going places together and snuggling at night and really taking care of each other."

"Would you want anyone else in our family?" I asked, although I already knew the answer to this one.

He nods his head vigorously, and his mouth breaks into a broad smile broadly. "A brother and sister," he said.

"What would you tell other kids, to help them, if they were in a single parent family?" I asked.

Dev suddenly stood. He put his hands on his hips, and his expression turned very serious. His voice was solemn and concerned as he said, "Don't worry. Don't just be sad. Just be happy. Just enjoy your single parent. Some day you'll get another parent. Trust me."

I couldn't help but grin, feeling proud of his composure and passion.

"Do you think we'll get another parent in our family some day?" I asked.

"Yes, we will," he said, confidently.

I was relieved, feeling comfortable with Dev's

understanding and acceptance of our life. I only wish I had the same strength of conviction to believe that someday it will be different.

Getting Ready to Date

Originally published in Our Times, *February 2003*

CB

When I got divorced I put the whole concept of dating on a shelf, in the back of a closet, in the basement. Frankly, the idea of dating held absolutely no appeal to me, on several different levels. First, there was the inevitable feeling you get when going through a divorce – all members of the opposite gender stink. Then there was the residual self-doubt and low self-esteem that come from a bad marriage. And finally, there was the minor detail that I was pregnant at the time.

With the birth of my son, thoughts of dating were even further from my mind. I was tired, sore, nursing, crying, covered in spit-up, and did I mention tired. I had a new-born baby, a full-time job, an endless supply of dirty laundry, and precious little help. I barely had the energy and brain cells to work, my conversation skills had been reduced to a series of monosyllabic sounds, and I wasn't keeping up with the people already in my life, so how could I let anyone new in.

The temptation to date washed over me quickly when Dev was four months old. I had somehow struck up one of those odd cyber-relationships where you communicate electronically and flirt at an abnormally safe distance. When the question of meeting "in-real-life" came up, I actually thought about it. For maybe one minute anyway, before Dev woke up from his nap crying, and my milk let down. Who was I kidding – I pushed thoughts of dinner, wine, and candle light back to the deep dark recesses of my mind and went on with my life.

The terrible-twos, potty training, and very emotional threes wiped me out. My life was filled with the many issues of a preschooler. Finger painting, a nasty biting phase (Dev was doing the biting, not me), "big boy" underwear, beach pails, and snow suits became all consuming. Thoughts of having a serious relationship with a man fleeted quickly through my mind on a quarterly basis, but being a mommy was all I could handle.

Right about the same time that I again began to think dating might be nice, Dev started to understand the concept that men and women, boys and girls, do in fact date. He made his newly acquired understanding, and feelings about dating, quite clear one day.

Out of nowhere, Dev announced, "I don't want you to ever go on a date, Mom."

"Why is that?" I asked, trying to keep my amusement from showing.

"Because," he explained. "If you date then you'll have to let some man kiss you, and that's not okay with me."

And there you have it. My favorite part of the dating game was now my beloved son's worst nightmare. Long gone were the days of dancing all night or catching live music at the local pub. It was no longer just about whether or not I was ready for a relationship. I had to worry about whether or not we were both ready.

Of course, there are all of the practical issues to deal with as well. The ever-growing laundry, homework, dishes, and mail — all of the piles that seem to grow uncontrolled in various corners of the house. Then there's the issue of babysitters, which are expensive and hard to schedule. And let's not forget the age-old predicament of finding a good guy, worth the effort involved with even one date. Gone also are the days of looking for someone who might be interested in kids "someday" because I have one at home today.

I gently explain to Dev that if we ever hope to have a dad in our family, it will have to start with me dating.

"I know," he says. "But what if we just get a brother first?"

The idea is actually tempting. I'm well established in the role of mommy now, and the role of significant-other seems foreign and difficult, at best. But when I look at the long list of things I want to provide for my son and myself, including healthy relationships and siblings, I hold onto the hope that someday we'll have it all.

Teammates Survive Their Separate Lives

Originally published in Our Times, *March 2003*

I started teaching art classes to children, at the Exeter Center for Creative Arts - a job I truly love. Interestingly enough, finding a job that I look forward to every day has also highlighted a number of issues for me as a single parent.

When I started the endeavor, it never occurred to me that Dev would have a jealousy problem regarding my new young friends. More than that, I never envisioned the lengths to which he might go to interrupt or join me in my new venture.

It started simply enough, with a few concerns, which perhaps I should have paid more attention to.

"You're too nice," Dev told me one day, after I had told him about my art lesson with a group to terrific preschoolers. "You're so nice to them, they're all going to start to like you."

I wasn't sure where this would go. It didn't sound like a

bad thing to me. "But I want them to like me," I said.

Dev moved closer to me, looking down. "Yeah…but what if they like you so much, you forget about me?"

It often hits me, with only two of us, how fragile our little family is. But I hadn't thought about Dev having the same feelings. From his point of view, with only one parent, the possibility of ending up alone must be quite scary. Of course, I assured him that I would never forget about him, no matter how much my new friends liked me.

With our new schedule came new childcare issues. I arranged for Dev to go into the after-school program for one day each week and to go to his cousins' house for another day. Since he had long wanted to stay after school and since he loves spending time with his cousins, this seemed like a great solution for both of us. And after extensive consideration, I decided I would bring him along to the art center for one of the classes, to cover the third day.

I worried about the effects of this new, busy, schedule impacting our routines and our time we spend together. Dev has always been particularly sensitive to times when my life gets busy and we don't have as much time for each other. We have become accustomed to the school day ending early enough for us to spend the majority of the afternoon together. With this new schedule, three of those afternoons were now affected.

I try to find other ways to make up for the missing time. We plan special activities for the days I'm not teaching and special dinners on the nights I am teaching. I give him tasks to help me during the class he attends, making him my teacher's assistant.

The first couple of weeks went off without a hitch. He loved after-care and the bonus time with his cousins, and we had a great time together at pottery class. It took no time for Dev to become familiar and comfortable with the art center, and make it a part of his life. He struts around, making sure we have enough stools for everyone and greeting the other kids as they show up. I let my guard down, feeling confident that I'd worked it all out.

And then, as another week started, he was sent home from school because he "didn't feel well." I was already off to the center and my sister fielded the call.

"I thought you'd come get me and bring me to your class," Dev said, when I spoke to him on the phone. "I thought I could go with you."

He was very disappointed to find that I couldn't pick him up and that I wouldn't bring him to class if he was sick. He spent the afternoon playing, running around, and snacking at my sister's house. That night, he did end up getting a fever, and I kept him home the next day.

Again, he played all day, occasionally asking me to bring him to school. And again, he was disappointed when I wouldn't bring him to pottery class that afternoon, repeating that he can't come if he's not feeling well. But he was also pleased to find that he would go back to his cousin's house.

On the third day of this cat-and-mouse game, he woke up looking well. But when I told him he had to get ready for school, he wrapped his arms around his belly, moaned, and said he didn't feel good.

"You have to go to school," I said. "You can't stay home every day, and I really have to work."

"Take me with you today," he pleaded.

"I can't," I said, feeling guilty. "But it's soccer day. I'll pick you up in time to go to soccer practice."

He seemed to think about that for a few minutes. "Can I go to Aunty Sue's house?" he asked. "Just until it's time for soccer?"

I shook my head no.

"But if I can't go with you," Dev started. "Why can't I go to Sue's?"

"You have to go to school," I said firmly. "That's your job. And that's how you can help me." He looked at me, and I could see his mind working on another line of defense. I continued quickly, "We're a team. You and me. It's my job to work and your job to go to school. And when we're both done with our jobs, I'll pick you up, and we'll go play soccer."

After a few moments, he hugged me tightly. "Okay, Mama," he said. "We're a team."

I wanted to scoop him up in my arms and keep him with me, day in and day out. I wanted to find a way to work this new found job I love and have more time with my boy. Instead, I explained to him that we both have things to do, but no matter where we are and what we're doing, we're a family and a team, and no one can change that.

Learning the Tricks of Traveling with Tots

Originally published in Our Times, *April 2003*

CB

I am addicted to travel. I have been for a long time. The ability to pack a few things in a backpack and take off for a weekend or a week is something I've always cherished. So, when I first faced the prospect of becoming a single mother, I couldn't help but worry - how would I continue to travel?

The issue of pulling together all the gear needed to take a child on a trip, or just out of the house, has been addressed on many television sit-coms. In reality, few of us would worry about packing the baby swing, high chair, and Exersaucer for a weekend away. But it's difficult to squeeze everything you need into one bag when it takes an entire suitcase just to carry the diapers.

Determined not to give up my favorite past time, I started immediately strategizing and conceptualizing. There had to be a way for one woman to travel with one child. As soon as Dev was able to sit up by himself, I whisked him off to the photo shop for his very own passport. We'd be ready, as soon as I had it all figured out.

We started small, taking day trips and over nights around New England. Each time I tried to pack lighter, using fewer bags, and lugging less gear. I tried to calculate the precise number of diapers we would need for the length of time we'd be gone - be it a few hours or a few days - trying to return home with no more than three unused. I also worked to figure out exactly how many items of clothing he'd need. Coming home with clean clothes and unused diapers meant a waste of packing space and energy.

I also developed a great system of hanging bags on the back of the stroller, balancing it just right so it wouldn't tip over. This proved to be a problem going through airport security, however, as everything had to be removed from the stroller, including the baby, and scanned separately.

Dev was one and a half when he got his first stamp in his passport. Although, for our first international trip, I didn't dare go it alone. Still, with my mother and sister ready to travel with us, countless people called me crazy.

"You're bringing a toddler to England?" they asked. This was usually followed by questions of why and how. The vacation was a smashing success - although I did come home with too many unused diapers.

When Dev was a toddler, we ran into a host of new problems. Airport security insisted that he walk through the gate by himself. I had to wait for a moment, after he passed through, before I could follow. Our bags stacked up at the end of the scanner and Dev took off down the gateway. On one trip, I left my purse at the gate because I was so preoccupied with catching Dev while not losing his blanket.

With each trip, I learned more about traveling with a child, and traveling with Dev. As he grew older, my worries about the logistics of traveling with a child changed to anxiety over whether or not Dev would pick up my travel bug or rebel against it. I was learning how to travel with my child, but would he continue to cooperate?

When Dev was three we went to Paris with my sister. This time, we didn't need to lug the suitcase full of diapers along, and I was feeling a little too confident with how well it was going. What I hadn't taken into consideration was Dev's changing needs. He wasn't an infant anymore, he was a preschooler. After we were kicked out of the Picasso Museum because Dev decided to scream, non-stop, at the top of his lungs in the middle of the museum, I knew I needed a new approach.

We developed a number of strategies together to help with our trips. Before each trip, Dev packs his own backpack of toys, books, and activities. We only spend part of each day touring, and part of each day is reserved for fun - running on a beach, tossing a football, or playing games. We've become experts at seeking out playgrounds. Whenever Dev is overtired or feeling homesick, we order room service and sit on the floor of our room for a "carpet picnic."

In the summer of 2001, Dev and I spent almost every

weekend traveling to and around Quebec province. This, unfortunately, was a bit more than Dev could handle.

"I never want to go to Canada again," Dev said a number of times. "The TV isn't in English, everyone speaks French, and the food is different. Nothing is the way I like it."

But how many four-year-olds know that, I wanted to ask him, although I knew he wouldn't care. I worried that I blew it. How would I continue to fulfill my passion for travel if my pint-sized travel partner wasn't going to be a willing participant? After all, one of the things I've learned along the way is that, with only one adult, it's hard enough dealing with all the paperwork and luggage, and getting from one place to the other, without also having to chase down and tackle a forty pound child at every turn.

We've taken a break from travel for the past year, in part due to circumstance and necessity, and in part to give Dev time off after our summer in Quebec. With each passing month, I grow more restless, wanting to run away to some distant land. All the while, I've tried to determine if Dev would be ready for another trip, unsure about how willing he'll be the next time I say, "we're going."

Then, out of the blue, Dev said, "Mama, I've been wondering. What will we do with the cats?"

"When?" I asked.

"What will we do with the cats the next day we go to Ireland?" Dev asked.

My heart skipped a beat. I felt like a kid that was just

given the key to the toy store. I had received the go-ahead, and we were free to move about the world again.

Our Differences

Originally published in Our Times, *May 2003, titled "Deriving, Defusing and Delighting in Our Differences".*

I've known from the beginning that Dev would be challenged by a host of differences that make him uniquely him. Secretly, I hoped that he would live his life unaware of these differences, oblivious and unquestioning. At least until he was old enough to understand and accept the diversity that makes up his life.

I don't know if it comes with being six years old or being in kindergarten, but we have entered into a new phase of social and self awareness. Of course, it was bound to happen - it's a part of growing up. I just thought, and hoped, we'd have more time. I wouldn't mind ten more years of obliviousness. But, as has always been the case with Dev, he has moved into this new phase long before I was prepared to deal with it.

Fighting back the fear that this is the door opening to a life-time of peer pressure and self-doubt, I try to help Dev accept and deal with the things he feels prevent him from fitting in.

Being half Mediterranean, in a family full of pale Irishmen, I worried that Dev would feel different from the rest of his large, extended family. I was relieved to find that his olive complexion, particularly rich in the summer, did not seem to be an obvious issue for him. It wasn't until he recently drew a self-portrait, giving himself brown skin, that I knew he fully realized his skin tone as one of the things that makes him different.

"I love your self-portrait," I said, trying to keep my voice light and casual. "I'm curious though. Why did you decide to use brown?"

He looked at me with his serious face before matter-of-factly saying, "Because my skin is kind of brown." He held his arm out next to mine. "See," he said. "I'm darker than you and all of my cousins."

I hugged him tight, nodding my head. "You did a great job on your self-portrait," I said again.

Then there is the issue of his name itself. His first name is rare, even in Ireland, but it is made even more unique with the addition of a Moroccan middle name.

"I want another name, a different name," he tells me. "Why can't I be called Aaron Carter? Or something else easy."

I explain what makes his name special and interesting, certain that he has tuned me out after the first few words.

With school and access to the "boy's room," Dev has also become suddenly aware of another physical difference between himself and many of the other boys. Without a father in the house to discuss this strictly male issue, we stumble around the topic.

"Are you upset that you're different from some of the other boys?" I ask.

"All of the other boys," he corrects me. "I'm different from all of the other boys."

"I know it seems like that," I sympathize. "But I promise you're not the only one." I try to explain my decision to keep him exactly as God made him, but I know he's too young for the details. "If we lived in Europe," I finally add in desperation. "You'd be just like all the other boys."

He nods his head, dismissing me, as if to say I can't possibly understand.

We have also spent a tremendous amount of time, throughout Dev's life, addressing the most obvious difference that he faces - his single-parent family. I made the distinction between father and dad, starting from a very young age, reinforcing that he has a father but that our family does not have a dad.

When he was four, he was able to explain this calmly to his friends, confidently answering their questions. Now, at six, when faced with the question of who his father is, Dev has adopted a new approach.

"I lied," he said quietly, unable to look me in the eye. "We were talking about fathers at school, and I said mine is named Mike."

I calmly asked him why he felt he needed to lie.

"I don't have a father," he said. "I don't even have a step-father. I just want to fit in. I don't want to be different any more."

The guilt of being the one who put Dev in this predicament defeated the impulse to lecture him on lying. Instead, we discuss alternative tactics for the next time the question arises, agreeing that he should talk about his grandfather rather than lying.

And for the sixth time that week, I launch into my little spiel about why everyone is unique, no two people are the same, and that he's really not as different as he feels. I try to assure him that his feelings are normal, and that most of his friends are, or will be, having these feelings as well. I talk again about the different kinds of families and point out other children we know who have single-parents. All the while, I push back thoughts that this is only the beginning.

The struggle to fit in and the overwhelming feelings of being different are certainly not unfamiliar or forgotten for most adults. As parents, we relive these insecurities and fears through the eyes of our children. And despite our current society, where the divorce rate is consistently high, it is hard not to feel like an oddity - for the single-parent, as well as the child.

Time to Grow the Brood and Geriatric Ovaries

CB

I'm not quite sure exactly when that familiar old urge for a gaggle of little boys started seeping into my subconscious. Suddenly it was there, like ghosts of a long-forgotten past, the echo of laughing children that only ever lived in my dreams. The cherished image of five little boys, hair wild, knees skinned, smeared with dirt, and good-humored shouts haunting my days.

Before I was fully aware of it, or perhaps before I was willing to admit it, I was back to reading books and magazines about infants and catching up on the latest philosophies for a healthy pregnancy. I started searching the sperm banks again, as I had years earlier, before getting married, before having Dev. I spent hours looking through descriptions of donors, wondering how difficult it would be to match Dev's unique look. And spent hours more searching more broadly, deciding that siblings didn't have to match.

Quickly nearing forty, I was no longer in my prime, but I was healthy, and as far as I could tell, everything was still working properly. I devoured all the information I could find on pregnancy later in life. There were complications of course, but I was not yet too old for pregnancy to be realistic and possible. My grandmother had been forty-four when she had my mother, her fourth child, which motivated me and strengthened my determination.

Dev had always wanted siblings, and I had always wanted multiple children. Besides, once you had one, how much more difficult could it be adding another? Dev was in school, and I was sure I could deal with a baby at home again. The time seemed perfect.

There was a lot more at risk this time, a lot more to consider. As I had done before, I thought about the potential donors I knew. The problems there were many. For starters, most of the men I knew were married. Most of those that weren't married, weren't suitable. There was also the issue of bringing an actual man into Dev's life. It wasn't just my heart on the line, or the heart of the future child, but also the heart of this amazing boy I loved more than everything.

It didn't take long to decide that this time the anonymity and emotional distance created by using a sperm bank was the only way to go. I also realized that moving forward with the assistance of a doctor was the most responsible approach to take. I had a child to take care of, and I didn't want to take any unnecessary risks. So, I scheduled an appointment with the doctor who had delivered Dev.

I was surprised at how nervous and uncomfortable I was discussing my plan and desire with the doctor. A small voice had started somewhere in the recesses of my mind, which I tried to ignore.

The doctor, of course, was patient and kind. He seemed neither surprised nor troubled by my desire to have a child as he explained the options available and process involved. He also explained the risks and concerns.

"You have geriatric ovaries," he said, in a painfully blunt manner.

I'm sure the shock showed on my face. I felt as though I had been slapped. I was not even forty years old. How could any part of me be considered 'geriatric'? The silence went on a bit too long, and that voice in the back of my mind was starting to grow louder.

"It's not impossible," the doctor finally continued. "But at this point we have to consider that your body and cycle are unpredictable and not necessarily working up to the most efficient level."

I nodded. A hot flush had spread across my cheeks, and my eyes felt pinned open as wide as they could grow. I wondered for a moment if I had gone into shock and half expected the doctor to jump into action over some concern for my health. I was geriatric, after all.

"We'll start you on some hormones," the doctor continued. His voice seemed more gentle, slower. "We'll start with Clomid, to increase ovulation and ensure you're on a predictable schedule."

He talked on for a few more minutes, but I was only able to hear half of what he said. I nodded and forced a smile, hoping I appeared confident, controlled. I focused on my breathing, certain that at any moment I would start to hyperventilate if I wasn't careful.

"I know searching the donor database is the part everyone enjoys," the doctor said, "but we'll get to that when we're closer to insemination time."

But that's the fun part, the part I want to do, I thought. Wasn't this all about picking out just the right features and creating my child? Suddenly, it all felt very complicated and very serious.

The doctor had moved on to discussing costs and the estimated expense of the whole process, most of which would not be covered by insurance. Again, I smiled and nodded, trying to present an image of total confidence and control, but inside I was beginning to panic. That voice in the back of my mind had started screaming at me, and it was getting harder to ignore.

I took the Clomid prescription from the doctor and agreed to schedule bloodwork. I assured him I understood the process we would follow and promised to call if I had any questions or problems. Then I shook his hand and thanked him for his time. I nodded and smiled at the staff and other patients as I wandered out of the offices and out of the building—nothing going on here, nothing to see. I concentrated on moving casually, but wanted to run out, get in my car and never look back.

Still, I filled the prescription and started taking the Clomid. I wanted another child. What wouldn't I do to make that happen? As the time came to do the bloodwork and follow up with the doctor, I had finally started to re-think the plan. That voice in my head was finally breaking through.

The fact was, it was going to be expensive to go through the whole process. Money had always been an elusive resource, and supporting my little family of two had always been a challenge. How would I manage to pay for the process, never mind ongoing support of a family of three?

Reluctantly, I had to admit that being told I had geriatric ovaries, geriatric eggs, had shaken my convictions. If my ovaries were old, how many tries at insemination would it take to get pregnant, and how much would that cost? If my eggs were old and somehow compromised, was I risking the health of a potential future child just by trying to get pregnant? It felt irresponsible.

Another fear had taken root as Dev and I went through our days, me with this secret, looking at everything we did, every moment of our lives, trying to visualize how it would change with a new baby in the mix. Everything would be different, for better and for worse.

The risks piled up, and my resolve waned. I had Dev, and we had a good life together. It wasn't always easy or smooth, but we loved each other, and our little family was happy and healthy. I no longer felt confident about risking it all. At my follow-up appointment, I told the doctor I changed my mind. He did not seem surprised, just as he had not been when I first met with him.

I left the doctor's office and sat in my care. I took several deep breathes. My heart felt like it was no longer beating regularly. Silently, tears spilled from my eyes and rolled down my cheeks. I grieved the loss of a child I never had and never would have. I tipped my head back against the headrest. The spring sun shone through and warmed my face. After a few minutes, I nodded at my reflection in the rearview mirror. I was Dev's mother, and that was enough. It was time to let the dream of a brood of boys go.

Independence is in the Eye of the Beholder

Originally published in Our Times, *June 2003*

CB

I saw a boy walking on Lafayette Road* recently, near the Portsmouth-Rye line. He couldn't have been more than eight years old, in a jacket and baseball cap - he seemed so small. He was all alone, walking slowly along the busy street, turning to look with each car that passed him.

My stomach knotted up instantly. What was he doing out there by himself, in so much traffic? Where were his parents? What if something happened to him?

After a moment, I realized I had slowed down significantly, trying to keep an eye on the small figure, reflected in my side mirror, who was kicking up dust and pebbles with each sneakered step. Honking from the cars behind me and Dev's persistent questions about what was going on brought my attention back to the road before me. I checked the mirror several more times, but the figure had faded from my view.

I scanned every parking lot and car I passed, looking for a police officer. Someone needed to check on the little guy. Someone needed to make sure he was going to be safe. I scolded myself for not bringing my cell phone with me when we left the house.

"Why are you so worried about him?" Dev asked me from the back seat. "He's being careful."

I couldn't help but wonder if this wasn't a way for Dev to ask why it is that I'm so strict with him. Especially, when there appears to be parents out there who let their children do all kinds of cool things.

"He's too young to be out here alone," I said. "He must be only eight years old."

"He's big," Dev countered. "He's older than me. He's big enough to be out by himself."

This has become an on-going issue between us, and I realize that the time has come for me to let go a little. But I don't want to.

Dev has barely left my sight his entire life. He's never been allowed to just go out and play, like many of the other kids in our neighborhood. I have always insisted that if he wanted to be outside playing, I had to be there with him, by his side, making sure he was safe.

But this summer, Dev is going to be six-and-a-half, as he loves to remind me. Too old for his mother to be tagging along behind him - according to him - and too young to be out there alone - according to me.

My vigilance, I know, is due in part to the craziness of

the world we live in. With stories of children being taken from their homes, yards, and playgrounds, constantly showing up in the news, it's hard to relax and let go. My vigilance is also due in part to our personal situation, with an absentee father who could show up at any moment.

But I have to admit, whether I want to or not, that my cautious attention to and obsession with Dev's security is due in large part to my own personal struggles over my abilities, or inabilities, to keep him safe. If I can see him then at least I have a shot at protecting him. At least, that's what I've always assured myself.

"Please, Mom," Dev pleads with me. "Please, can I go out and play ball."

"I must be able to see your body," I say seriously. I don't want him to realize the anxiety that spreads quickly through me. "If I look outside, I better be able to see you."

With spring finally upon us, and the sun warming the air at long last, Dev and I have come to a new understanding. I allow him to go into the back yard as long as I can see him. Not the side yards. Not the front yard. Not the neighbor's yard or the street where all the other kids play. Just our yard and the adjoining backyard of the neighbor's house.

There's a part of me that welcomes this new phase in our lives, when he can be more independent, and I can have more time to get things done. There's also the pride in watching your child grow and enter into these new phases with excitement and confidence.

"Thanks, Mom," Dev yells, already half way down the

back steps.

Of course, he takes to this new way of life quite easily. He chats with the man next door, asking him to join in a game of yard hockey, and connects with the pack of neighborhood boys that run from one end of the yard to the other like a bunch of wild wolf pups.

I, on the other hand, continue to struggle with this new arrangement. My breath catches if I don't see him instantly when I look outside, and my mind immediately wanders to the worst possible scenario if I haven't heard his voice or laugh for too long. I am still not able to accomplish anything. Instead, I sneak from one window to the next, hiding in the shadows and behind curtains, keeping a watchful eye out.

Little does he know, he has not yet gained the independence he so eagerly wants. But he's outside, and he's with the guys. And what I do with my time is of no concern to him, I'm sure.

---

* Lafayette Road is a busy section of Route 1 that runs along the seacoast of New Hampshire. In this section, traffic is always an issue, with many cars turning in and out, along the endless line of car dealerships, restaurants, offices, and shops.

Heading to Camp for First Summer Vacation

Originally published in Our Times, *July 2003*

CB

The benefits of having school aged children are far reaching. For most of the year, the kids are occupied, challenged, and shaped in a safe and, hopefully, fun environment. They learn the building blocks needed to survive and thrive, while developing interpersonal skills and making friendships that may last a lifetime. The drawback, however, to having a school aged child is enough to make a parent crazy - it's summer vacation.

When I think about the summer vacations of my own childhood, I remember days on end spent at the beach or the pool, running around the neighborhood in packs, catching turtles in the creek, and tense games of kickball in the cul-de-sac. Summer vacation was a time that we waited for with anticipation and excitement. My nostalgia for these long-gone months of freedom sometimes gets the better of me, and I overflow with enthusiasm for Dev's impending break. But it never takes long for reality to come rushing back in.

I, like most of my friends while I was growing up, had a stay-at-home mom. There was never an issue or question when it came to summer break. Everyone I knew did the same thing. There may have been a family vacation or two, but almost everyone was home for the season. And, although I'm sure there were camps available, I can't recall there ever being a discussion over who was going to what camp and which one's to register for.

In today's world, stay-at-home moms have become few and far between. For a single mom, staying home with the kids, even for part of the year, is a luxury that's usually impossible. But when you have a job to go to all summer long, what do you do with the kids?

It was easy while Dev was in day care. It was a non-issue. He just stayed in day care all year round, winter and summer, snow and sun. I was free to take care of our lives and work my job, secure in the knowledge that he was well taken care of, continually nurtured, and having fun.

This summer is different. As Dev completes his first year of "real school" and starts his first real summer vacation, I have been plagued with the question of what to do with him for the next two and a half months.

The options are seemingly endless; almost to the point of making the issue more difficult than helpful. A little research with local organizations, newspapers, and other parents, yields a startling list of available summer time diversions for children of all ages. There are nature-oriented camps on the river and ocean, art and music camps, sports camps for every sport, computer camps, reading camps, scout camps, and generalized camps that do a little bit of everything.

"I want to go to soccer camp," Dev says. "And a camp where I can canoe, and another sports camp."

"We'll see," I reply. "Maybe we'll pick one."

Unfortunately, a lot of these camps are quite costly, which for a single-parent, single-income family can be a show-stopper. They also have a tendency to fill up quickly, making it difficult to get the dates and times needed.

Many working and single parents start planning the summer camp schedule months early, long before the New England snow has melted. This is a lesson that new-to-the-summer-vacation parents learn quickly. You have to start planning and register early if you want to get a spot.

One single mother I know has the summer camp routine down to a science. Starting in early spring, when summer is still a foggy dream for many people, she begins the calling, planning, and scheduling. Except for two or three weeks, each summer, when they take vacation together, her son participates in one camp after another, getting a mix of arts and culture, sports and nature, and just plain fun. She coordinates the dates and registration forms, and spends nearly as much money for summer camps as for the whole school year at private school.

But the question remains, if you can't afford a summer full of camps and still have to go to work every day regardless of what month it is, what do you do with your child? Other people I know have taken to "nanny sharing" for the summer, and I considered this option for a while. If you can find a temporary nanny, available for the summer months, this can work out great. Some high school and college students are up for this challenge. The cost, when shared with other families, is usually reasonable and your children get to stay in familiar surroundings while still having other kids to play with.

In the end, however, Dev and I lucked out. We will both be spending our first real summer vacation in camp together, all summer long - me as the teacher, and Dev as the camper. I am grateful for this opportunity that most working parents do not get. I will go to work every day, and he will come with me. But instead of being locked up in a stuffy office, we will play games, do art, and eat Popsicles - together. And, just maybe, we'll find time to hunt for turtles.

Finding Time for Self

Originally published in Our Times, *August 2003*

 C3

In the single-parent household, it falls on that parent to be all and do all. The single mother, or single father, must be both mother and father, housekeeper and cook, best friend and disciplinarian, bread winner and nanny. With all that needs to be done, all that needs to be taken care of, one question bubbles to the surface - if the single parent is taking care of everything else, who is taking care of the single parent?

Caring for and nurturing ourselves is often the hardest thing for many of us to do. For me, it is difficult, and frequently impossible, to remember that I too must be cared for. When I'm loading dirty laundry into the washing machine at midnight, trying to catch up on the dishes at seven a.m. before rushing out to work, or answering Dev's call for "Mama!" for the hundredth time, the last thing on my mind is what my own needs might be.

Paradoxically, when you most need to care for yourself is exactly when you have the least amount of time to take care of yourself. The busier you are, the more overworked you are, the more you need to take time for yourself. Never an easy task.

Caring for myself in the face of all the other things that demand my attention and time is an issue that I continue to struggle with. However, I've tried to take some tips from women I know who are skilled at caring for themselves.

Start Your Mornings Right - Develop a ritual for the morning, to start your day right. It should be something that relaxes you and gets your spirit, creativity, and energy flowing. Try yoga style stretches or writing freely in a journal before getting out of bed. Some mornings, I like to just lay in bed, awake, listening to the silence in the house.

Pamper Yourself as Often as You Can - If you take care of yourself, you will feel better about everything. Treat yourself well. Indulge in the things you love. Home spa items can be wonderfully relaxing and affordable. A hot bubble bath, a glass of wine, and scented candles go a long way to give the feeling of extravagance.

Give Yourself Time-Outs - When things start to get out of control or you feel yourself getting frustrated, give yourself a time out. Take a little break, count to ten, and breathe deeply. Tell the kids that you need a few minutes alone and send yourself to your room for five or ten minutes.

Accept That Not Everything Will Get Done - There's

only one of you, and you can't possibly get it all done. The sooner you accept that some things will have to go undone, the less stress you will have. Try not to think about the extra pile of laundry that is gathering or the blanket of toys that spills out of the kids' rooms.

Take the Night Off - It is far too tempting to keep plucking at all the chores for as long as your legs will carry you and your eyes can be propped open. But all work makes a very grumpy parent. Make it a point to save your evenings for relaxing pastimes that you enjoy, like watching movies, reading, or doing crafts. Even if you only keep a couple evenings for yourself, you'll be far better off for it.

Get Some Sleep - Never underestimate the restorative power of sleep. If you are lucky enough to get your kids to take a nap, join them. Get to bed as early as you can, and sleep as late as you can.

Do What You Love - If there is a particular hobby or pastime that you really love to do, do it. Schedule it into your life. Write it on the calendar in pen so that it can't be erased. Whatever it may be, it is important to spend time doing things that you absolutely love to do.

Balance is Key - Find a balance between your needs and your child's, work and home, obligations and fun. If your life is in balance, you will feel more satisfied and far less resentful of any sacrifices you need to make.

Laugh as Often as Possible - Nothing boosts the energy and spirit like a good, hearty, laugh. Best yet, laugh with your children, long and hard. Try having a tickle-fest. You'll all feel better and for that moment all of the work and responsibility will fade.

The Summer That Didn't Work

Originally published in Our Times, *September 2003*

CB

As summer draws rather quickly to a close, and the school year is just around the corner, I can't help but review the past couple of months with a touch of disappointment. Don't get me wrong, Dev and I have had a good summer. But it's hard not to think about how it could have been different, could have been better.

I've been fortunate this year, working in a job that made it possible and practical to bring Dev to work with me. Not only have we been able to spend most of the summer together, but he's also been able to spend it with other kids, working on fun projects, and gaining a bit of cultural enrichment along the way.

On the other hand, we've been busy. More accurate is to say that I've been busy — straight out, crazy, can't keep up with anything, busy — going from teaching all day, to working through emails while cooking dinner, to writing all night after Dev goes to bed. The weekends have been no easier, between catching up with the ever growing "to do" list, running errands, family obligations, and yet more work. And then there are the endless chores involved with taking care of a home that I just don't keep up with. Summer has been anything but a vacation this year.

As I finished up at work the other day, cleaning off my desk and listening to the voice mail, Dev waited somewhat less than patiently.

"Please don't touch the copier," I said, for the fourth or fifth time.

"When are we going?" he asked, also for the fourth or fifth time.

I walked through the art center, closing windows, turning off lights, and washing out paint brushes. I double checked the registration for the next day and listened to voice mail one last time. Finally, I picked up the car keys and told Dev it was time to go.

"But you don't have your bag," he said, staring in disbelief at the over stuffed gray messenger bag that I have come to live out of, which still rested in its spot on the floor behind my desk. "Why aren't you bringing home your bag?"

"I thought I'd leave it at work tonight," I said. "I was thinking I'd just spend the evening with you and not work."

"Not work?" Dev asked. He looked at me sideways, as though he didn't quite understand what I was saying. "Not work at all? Not even a little bit?"

I shook my head from side to side. "Not even a little bit. Not tonight."

Dev smiled broadly, singing and skipping his way to the car.

That's what was missing, the carefree, relaxing days of summer. We had reached the end of the season but had not taken a vacation, not kicked back to enjoy the warm weather or long days and had not yet gone camping. We had only made it to the beach a handful of times and had still not found time for our one and only annual trip to Water Country.

I am not alone in this modern day, barely there summer. With most parents working, whether in a single- or two-parent family, it's hard to find the time to enjoy summer vacation with our kids. We scramble around, trying to give our children as much summer fun as we can, squeezing out a day here or there to enjoy it with them.

Frustrated by our lack of summer freedom, I made a list of all of the things I wished I had made time for, all of the things I wished Dev and I had been able to do in his few short months between kindergarten and first grade: a dinner picnic on the beach, lakeside camping, learning to ride a two-wheeler, fishing, baseball, s'mores, berry picking, eating lobsters, and star gazing. There are many more, but summer is short even if you aren't busy. With any luck, over the coming year, I'll manage to fix our lives so that next summer can be a vacation, which I'll gladly enjoy with my boy.

The Holidays are Coming

Originally published in Our Times, *October 2003*

❧

Neighborhoods are conspicuously quiet and empty in the middle of the day. Streets are moving slower, morning and afternoon, bogged down by swarms of large yellow busses. School is back in session and cool, crisp mornings have finally rolled in. All signaling the approach of the holiday season.

For many people, single and married, parent and not, the holidays are an odd mix of excitement and dread. Many anticipate the social aspects of the holidays, the celebrations and reenactment of beloved traditions. Many others, children in particular, look forward to the endless treats that come with the holiday season - from bags of candy, to tables of pies, to presents, presents, and more presents.

Unfortunately, for many of us, especially those of us that are single parents, the holiday season also means a lot more stress in our already insane lives. The holidays, from October through the next New Year, bring increased work and increased expenses.

Halloween is usually a fun and thrilling time of year. We always look forward to the excitement and creativity involved in creating a costume.

"What do you want to be for Halloween," I asked Dev, not long ago.

"A gargoyle," he responded quickly.

My mind began to race, trying to figure out an easy and cheap way to put together a gargoyle costume. He already has a gray sweat suit, I thought, but I'll need to make wings.

"Or maybe a scientist," Dev continued. "Or an army man." Hours later he said, "Maybe I should be a hockey player instead."

We decided to think about it some more and make our choice later.

Another issue that stumps me, every year at Halloween, is how to hand out candy and go trick-or-treating at the same time. I always consider just leaving the bowl of candy out for the hordes of costumed children that are sure to clamber by, but I'm afraid it will be gone too quickly. In the end, I try to find someone without children to do the handing out while I take Dev around the neighborhood.

Halloween also brings the annual questions regarding whether or not ghosts and witches exist, what will we do if a bat flies into our house, and if black cats really are bad luck. I imagine that the root of these questions stems from Dev's need to feel secure in our family and home. Of course, it could just be the spooky stories that prevail at this time of year.

Even with the joy and laughter that accompany it, I'm generally happy when the holiday passes, taking October with it, and allowing November to lumber in.

Thanksgiving is a welcome chance to enjoy the holiday season, surrounded by family and tradition, with less of the work and anxiety that accompany Halloween before it and Christmas after it. With Thanksgiving, our biggest worry is what kinds of pies to make, ensuring that everyone gets their favorites, and not missing Santa Claus in the Macy's Thanksgiving parade.

Christmas is another story all together. The work can become overwhelming and the expense unbearable. Still, I can't help being seduced by the festivity, Christmas carols, and bright lights everywhere. Christmas time traditions have always been some of my favorite.

The hardest part of Christmas, at least if you are tool-challenged as I am, is figuring out how to put the Santa gifts together. I try for gifts that don't require assembling, but inevitably they still require batteries and having to remove the ridiculous little screws to open the panel on the back. The worst, however, are the dozens, and sometimes hundreds, of tiny stickers that now come with everything. I once tried to pass off the stickers as a separate and bonus prize, but Dev complained that the toy didn't look like it did on the commercials. So, I still ended up spending the better part of an hour peeling and sticking.

Each year, I think about the one before, what worked well and what didn't, what gave me the most stress and what made my life easier. I try to come up with new ways to simplify our holiday season, make it smoother and more enjoyable. And each year, I try to think of new traditions to start that will make the holidays more meaningful and bring us closer during this stressful time.

Longing for the Men's Room

Originally published in Our Times, *November 2003*

ॐ

As a single mother of a son, it seems that some of our biggest struggles have always revolved around bathroom issues.

Even before the potty training and long before Dev was aware of his boy-ness, there were problems. In the beginning, the problem was how I would manage to get to the bathroom when we were out-and-about together.

A friend of mine, a married mother with a brand-new baby girl, was recently going on a road trip, just her and the baby. She was hoping to make the three-hour drive without having to stop. I told her she was lucky, at least the baby is still small enough to be in the car seat carrier.

When Dev was a baby, it was so easy to carry him, strapped snuggly in the carrier, and put him down in the stall while I answered nature's call. Road trips were practically effortless.

The trouble came when he got too heavy for me to haul him in the carrier. My choices were very limited; I wasn't going to put him down on the floor of the bathroom. I ended up getting a small stroller that quickly snapped open, then I'd wheel him in, and we'd wait for the large handicap stall, the whole time feeling both relieved and guilty for using the designated stall.

During the toddler years, bathroom breaks became a circus filled with Dev wiggling out of the stroller, trying to escape under the stall walls, and my constant shouts of "Don't touch that."

In an airport restroom one day, I was desperate. The large handicap stall was out of order and locked shut. Dev was in his stroller and not in the least bit trustworthy, so I couldn't let him out. And the stroller wouldn't fit in the smaller stall. I thought about waiting until we were back on the plane, but after quickly doing the math it didn't seem probable. I looked around at the women coming and going, rushing around the restroom, trying to decide what to do. After awhile, I noticed another mother, corralling two children at the sinks and helping them wash their hands.

"Could I trouble you?" I started, pointing at Dev, who was struggling against the belts of his stroller.

She smiled and nodded. "No problem," she said.

I felt confident that Dev was safe – surely, she wouldn't want another to watch after. Still, I moved as quickly as I could.

As Dev got bigger, and after he was potty trained,

bathroom predicaments eased off for a time. He stopped trying to make a break for it, waiting patiently while I had my turn, and got a thrill from having his turn.

That changed when Dev began to realize there was a different bathroom for men and women.

"Is this the women's?" Dev asks, every time we venture to the restrooms.

"Of course," I always answer.

"But I really want to use the man's room," Dev pleads.

"You can't," I say. "You have to stay with me."

"But there might be girls in there," Dev says.

And, in fact, we do have a problem if there are girls in the bathroom when we enter. Dev looks down and rushes along the wall in search of an empty stall, avoiding all eye contact with the dreaded beings of the opposite gender.

"Make sure no one comes in," he orders, as though I must obey him as payment for putting him through this humiliation.

Whenever possible, I allow him to use a different stall from me or wait for me outside of the stall, as long as I can always see his shoes. But with all that goes on in the world, I can't bring myself to let him go into the men's room by himself. Even in places that seem like they should be safe, I can't bring myself to let him go.

Dev loves the times when we are out with one of the men in his life - his grandfather, his uncles, and his friends' fathers. He jumps at every opportunity to talk them into bringing him to the men's room. For Dev, one of the highlights of starting real school was the ready access to the boy's room - a girl free sanctuary.

Another cherished right of being male, that Dev has grown to love, is the ability to relieve himself outside. This is clearly not something I'll ever grow to appreciate.

As we explored Odiorne Point State Park, on a beautiful, crisp fall day recently, ducking around bushes and under trees, Dev turned onto a barely visible path.

"Can I, please?" he asked, smiling and looking from me to a nearby bush. "I really have to. I really do."

"Fine," I nodded, continuing slowly down the path.

"Yeah," he said. He hummed and sang as he did his business.

When he caught up to me, he was singing and grinning widely. It was the ultimate men's room, I thought. And the perfect finishing touch to a great day out.

I frequently try to imagine how I'll handle this issue as he gets bigger and older, and I'm still at a loss. For a while, we will continue on as we are, trying to afford each other as much privacy and respect as we can, but keeping safety in the forefront. And maybe, some day soon, it will no longer be an issue we'll have to consider.

The Spirituality of Parenting

Originally published in Our Times, *December 2003*

A mother's day is a study in spirituality, faith, and trust in the universe. Being a parent requires a very close working relationship with powers far beyond any of this world.

My own journey to motherhood, and single-motherhood as it turned out, has been a test of faith from the beginning. It started with resolute prayers for a long-desired baby, followed by forty-two weeks of desperate prayers for that baby to be healthy. And as Dev grew, the pleas and prayers grew with him.

"If I can just survive until he's three," I prayed.

And then, "Please help me make it until he's four."

Most of our days start with blissful gratitude, as Dev climbs into bed with me, snuggling up close until the stiff curls on his head tickle me awake. I kiss his forehead and squeeze my eyes shut, silently thanking God for giving me this gift.

Rushing around the house in the dawn light, searching for clothing and shoes, and gathering all that is needed for the day, my prayers of gratefulness are replaced by a more desperate cry.

"Please," I pray to Dev. "Please put your shoes on. Please put your belt on. Please pack your backpack."

My appeals are met with a song and a dance, but not a whole lot of cooperation.

"Please, Dev," I continue my prayer. "Get ready for school."

Arriving at school, I am only allowed to kiss and hug Dev goodbye if I get it in quickly, beside the car, where there is little chance of any of "the guys" seeing me. After all, he's in the first grade now and image is already everything. I curse the universe for letting him grow up so quickly, ignoring the pre-school years when I had begged for him to grow up faster, and mourn the loss of my baby boy, who couldn't get enough hugs from his mother.

As he joins his friends and files into the school I say to myself, "Please keep him safe and give him a good day." On Fridays I add, "Please help him with his spelling test."

With every story on the news, every article that I read, and every movie that seems to hit too close to reality, a new flood of petitions bursts forth. I don't think it's possible to ask the universe for all the help that is needed in the twenty-first century world. Still I try, as I drive to work or back to the school to pick up Dev.

"Please protect him and keep him safe."

"Help him stay away from drugs."

"Let him grow up smart and honest."

"Please help me to do my best by him."

"Please let him be happy."

"Please…"

"Please…"

Away from him, with each of us leading our separate lives and Dev ensconced safely in his school, I find myself talking to God about other issues and asking the universe for assistance in ways beyond the immediate. I pray that I'm moving in the right direction, making the right decisions, and doing my best by Dev. I hope that everything will work out, that our bills will get paid, and that I'll manage to give my son a happy and fun Christmas. I ask for assistance for my family and friends, a cousin in Iraq, a sick aunt, a teenage godson, a friend going through a terrible custody battle.

More often than not, I pray for a week to end and a schedule free weekend to begin. "I just need one day to sleep in," I say to the universe. "Just one day."

I'd love to ask the universe to send someone to help me get the laundry and dishes done, someone to help Dev do his homework when I haven't finished my own work yet, someone to watch movies with late at night after Dev's asleep. But these feel like frivolous prayers, so I push them aside and load the washing machine while Dev eats his dinner.

As the day ends, Dev snuggles up next to me on the sofa. He picks up my arm and drapes it over his shoulder, holding on tight, humming quietly while he sucks his thumb. I push thoughts of our busy lives out of my head and savor the warmth and musky smell of my son, pressed up close to me. Again, I kiss his forehead and grin as the curls tickle my nose, and I thank God for this gift.

The Age of the Sleepover

ℭℬ

One of the hardest parts of being a parent is learning how to let go and give your child his or her independence. This is, perhaps, even harder for a single parent, when there is only you and your child, and the interdependency tends to be strong. It took a long while before I could comfortably let Dev go outside in the yard, and then the neighborhood, on his own, without me watching his every move, like a spy hiding behind the curtains, peering out the windows.

And then, the sleepovers started.

The first sleepover invitation came from a friend in his class at Catholic school. I knew the family well, knew their values and priorities, that there were no weapons or drugs in the house, and knew he'd be watched over, perhaps even more so than he would be at home. Still, as the evening went on, and he was conspicuously missing from our home, I found it hard to relax. My baby boy was out in the world without me. I kept wondering what he was doing and found it discomforting that I couldn't just go peek in on him.

More sleepover invitations came, on a regular basis, and every time I wanted to say no. I remembered sleepovers from my own childhood—nights filled with games, junk food, gossip, silly stories, and laughter. I wanted that for Dev. But I wasn't thrilled with him being off at other people's houses, away from me. Mostly, when I went to sleep, I wanted to know he was in the next room, tucked soundly in his bed. I wanted to be able to slip in, pull his covers up, and whisper "Mama loves you" in his ear.

Of course, the perfect solution would have been to host the sleepovers at our house. But, maybe because I was a single parent in a single income household or because there was always more to do than I could keep up with, our living circumstances never leant themselves to hosting sleepovers. Our apartments have always been too small and cluttered, our belongings often still in moving boxes and unorganized, even a year after moving in, and my housekeeping skills have always been painfully lacking.

When Dev was seven, and my parents were off on a trip, we borrowed their condo. Dev held his first sleepover with three of his friends. The boys arranged themselves in the lower level den, while I slept upstairs on the living room couch. We had plenty of junk food and several movies, and I laid awake listening to their chatter. At eleven one of the boys decided he didn't want to stay, and I called his parents, who were not surprised and happily came to get him. I was envious because Dev never wanted me to rescue him in the middle of a sleepover.

As Dev grew older and moved from Catholic school to public school, he made new friends that I didn't know. I didn't know their parents, didn't know anything about their households, values, or beliefs. With each sleepover invitation, I cringed and hesitated, listened to my instincts, and tried to weigh the risks with his happiness. A part of me wanted to say that I didn't care if he was happy or not; I didn't want to let him go. I spoke with parents on the phone, apologetically asking if they had firearms in the house, and met parents in driveways and parking lots to try and get a feel for whom I was trusting with my child's welfare.

There were times I said no, finding excuses to keep Dev from being too disappointed, but more often than not, I agreed to the sleepovers and spent the nights restlessly hoping someone was taking care of him, anxious for it to be over, so I could have Dev home again. Just as I got used to his occasional sleepovers with people I barely knew, we entered a new and more worrisome phase.

As Dev approached the teenage years, he made new friends at middle school, and there was no realistic way for me to know their parents. He asked to spend the night with kids I had only heard of through his wild tales, whose parents I had never spoken to and knew in no way at all. He was having sleepovers with virtual strangers, and I had to learn to trust that he would be okay. It was tough, but slowly, sleepover by sleepover, I began to relax.

One evening, when he was fourteen, he called to check in and informed me that he was not sleeping at the friend's house he had originally planned to but would be sleeping at "Pete's". Who the heck was Pete? Where did Pete live? I had dropped him off at a house, and that was the house I was holding in my mind as the visual image of where my child was. But he wasn't there. Dev assured me that Pete did not live far from the original destination, that all was okay with Pete's parents, that there were eight boys spending the night, they'd already been well fed, and he'd be back at the original house in the morning, before I was scheduled to pick him up. On the verge of a nervous breakdown and knowing that I had lost all control over my son's activities, I relented and hung up the phone.

I spent an anxious night not knowing exactly where, in an approximate three-mile radius, my son was or who he was with. I nearly crawled right out of my skin. With very little sleep and two large cups of coffee, I collected Dev in the morning, right where he said he'd be, thankful he appeared unharmed. Mustering the sternest tone of voice I could, I insisted that this scenario would not be happening again, but I knew it was useless. He was too happy; he'd had too much fun.

With summer upon us, the sleepovers continued more frequently than ever. Each week, I found myself home alone one night, while he made himself at home at a friend's house. We reached a new modus operandi, however. The plan had to be set ahead of time, to sleepover with a friend I was familiar with, and he had to check in before dark and first thing in the morning. Though he came home sick to his stomach, smelling of cigarette smoke, unfed and starving, and covered in poison ivy at different times throughout the summer, he inevitably came home happy every time.

I learned to relax with those nights alone, cooking meals he would not eat anyway, watching romantic comedies, and enjoying the quiet. But I always listened for the phone to ring, waiting for the call that would say he needed me to come get him, though I knew that call would probably never happen.

Moms Can Camp

છ

I have always loved camping. Maybe because, growing up in a family of seven, most of our vacations were spent camping in one forest or another, by a lake or river, and usually in an enormous tent. My childhood memories are punctuated with camping adventures that stayed with me.

This was something I wanted to give Dev as well. Camping provides an opportunity for connection with nature and adventure that comes as close to survivalism as most of us will ever get. Camping is work and fun, exercise and relaxation, with a lot of fresh air and dirt involved. I generally try to ignore the aspect of camping that involves creatures, as if not thinking about it means it won't be real.

The prospect of camping as a single mother with a young boy was daunting and seemed to exacerbate many of the logistical issues we already had. First there was the ever-present issue of bathrooms. How was I to use the bathroom and take a shower, without leaving Dev alone in the tent or forcing him to wait in the woman's room? Would he be safe in the men's room on his own? And, while I'm not usually prone to paranoia or excessive fear, I wasn't at all sure about the safety level for a single mother and a little boy sleeping alone in a tent in the woods.

When I proposed the idea of camping to Dev, he looked at me with that all-too-familiar you've-got-to-be-kidding-me expression. He didn't have to voice the question; it was the same look he gave me when I proposed anything potentially physical or adventurous. I knew what he was saying and asking just from the tilt of his head, the narrowed eyes, and the slightly cocked lips. "You want us to go camping? How are we going to do that? How are you going to do that? Moms don't camp." I couldn't blame him, really. I've never been known for my physical abilities. I'm not athletic, with poor hand-eye coordination, not exactly competent with tools, and I consistently struggled to start a fire in our fireplace. Could I set up a camp site, erect a tent, work a propane camp stove, and start a campfire?

Like with many other aspects of life, I was determined not to let my single-mother status stop me from living the way I wanted and providing Dev with the experiences I wanted him to have. For our first camping trip, I decided that there would be security—both psychological and physical—in the company of others. I did some research and found that the Sierra Club organizes group camping trips, including one to

Cape Cod. I joined and booked us on a week-long family camping trip with a group of other Sierra Club members, who we had never met before.

The trip was a success. I was comfortable leaving Dev alone in the tent from time to time, knowing our tent was surrounded by other families in our group, and he cooperated by staying in there when I asked him to. We managed to swim, hike, go on a whale watch, and have fun, and we made some new friends. Of course, being in a group, on a sponsored trip, we weren't totally on our own or self-sufficient. We did not have to worry about making a fire or keeping the camp stove running long enough to cook dinner, but I learned a few good tricks for our next attempt.

The next two times we went camping were in Quebec Provence, Canada, while we were touring and researching the travel guide I was writing. Both times I found family campgrounds, chock-full of French speaking children in all sizes and ages. Risking a higher noise factor, and potentially other unpleasantness, I asked for a spot near the bath houses each time. The proximity meant I could do what I had to quickly, without being too far from Dev for too long. And I reasoned that the higher traffic around our not-so-private camp site made us safer. Still, I had our wood baseball bat tucked into our tent beside my sleeping bag, for safety.

Each of the Quebec camping trips were only one night and more about work than vacation, but I readily counted them each a success. I'd managed the camp stove to feed us, and we'd slept safe and sound in our tent. I hadn't even attempted the campfire, but that was fine.

For our next camping adventure, I wouldn't say I was feeling exactly confident, but I was feeling ready. I wanted true wilderness, in the woods, with a river or lake, and no other campers immediately upon us. The same fears and self-doubt haunted me, but I was ready to conquer them. The biggest issue that remained, which I wasn't sure I could overcome, was the safety concern. It still felt uncomfortable and unsurmountable to be a single woman with a young child all alone in the middle of a forest. To overcome this, I invited my sister and her kids to join us. Looking back, clearly two women alone in the woods with kids probably made no more sense than just one, but I reasoned there was strength-in-numbers, so people say.

It was late in the season, promising a quieter campground, warm days, and cool nights. The owner of the campground offered us a bundle of firewood from under the deck, which we took, thankful we didn't have to pay for it or search for logs in the forest. We got a site right next to a small river, with a private beach, surrounded by trees, with no other campers on either side of us. With all four kids helping, we managed to set up the site in quick time, using a small tent as a sort of dressing room with our bags and a larger tent, filled wall -to-wall with air mattresses for sleeping. Before long we were swimming at our own beach. We walked up river with inner tubes and floated back down to our campsite. My sister and I lounged on the pebble covered beach, soaking in the sun, as the kids played in the water, leaping from a leaning tree into a still pool of warm water formed by the tree's tangled roots and limbs.

After a time, the kids' joyful screeching turned to panicked shrieks. The small gang flooded toward us, all talking excitedly at the same time, so that it took a while to figure out what was wrong. It wasn't until my nephew turned around, revealing a slimy black streak behind his knee that we understood the problem—leaches. After a few long moments of pure disgust, my sister and I armed ourselves with a salt shaker and tissue, removing the creature from my nephew's leg. By the time we had removed leaches from each of the children, we banned jumping into any standing water and sent all the kids to the tents to fully inspect their bodies for any more unwanted hitchhikers.

The next challenge came when we tried to settle in for the night, and one of the kids vomited, not quite getting out of the tent in time. My sister, as it was one of her children, gathered the blanket that had caught the assault, and brought it down to the river to wash it out. The rest of us waited, gathered closely together and silent while we listened for any signs of trouble. When the blanket had been rinsed and hung on a tree and my sister was safely back in the intimacy of our tent, we turned off the flash lights and settled into our sleeping bags. It could not have been ten minutes later when we heard rustling in the bushes and several large splashes in the river. There would be no more leaving the tent at night.

I had mastered the camp stove, making coffee, pancakes, eggs, and toast for breakfast, hot dogs and burgers for dinner. Each evening, we did our best to get a campfire going, though they never quite caught and barely threw enough heat to toast the marshmallows. Sedated by the cool evening air, the kids settled early each night, so the less-than-impressive fires weren't that big of a deal.

After a couple of days of swimming and sunning, we decided to take a drive around the mountains and see a few sights. With all the kids dressed in real clothes, shoes on for the first time in days, snacks and picnic lunch packed in a cooler, we headed for the car. The van door would not open. My sister pushed buttons and tried the handle to no avail. Puzzled and wondering if the kids had somehow broken the car, she climbed in the driver side and attempted to start it. Nothing. That was when we realized that using the remote to open and close the sliding door and hatch for several days had drained the battery, and a jump-start from AAA was required.

On our last night, we walked across the campground on our nightly run to the bath houses before settling in. We moved slower, enjoying the air a bit more, listening to the river, and talking about our week. As we passed one of the few other campsites in use, my niece looked over at the roaring campfire and stopped to stare for a few moments.

"Mom," she said, "why is our fire always just pink, and theirs is yellow and orange?"

My sister and I laughed, but I had to admit I felt the sting of failure. I was determined to end the trip with a roaring fire so strong the marshmallows would turn quickly to ash right on their sticks. As soon as we were back to the campsite, I turned all my attention to the fire, sending the kids into the woods several times for small sticks I might use as kindling. I put several wads of paper under the pile of twigs, put on a couple of small wedges of log, and lit it. A small flame flickered and danced on the paper. Smoke spiraled into the darkening sky. And then nothing.

I collapsed a cracker box and rolled it into a make-shift log, sticking it under the wood. This time, I used several matches, lighting the paper and cardboard in multiple places. It sputtered to life, the papers fully igniting and catching the small sticks. I watched the flames feeling good about my efforts, for a brief moment convinced I had succeeded. Then, I watched the flames falter and shrink. I blew on it lovingly, knowing I was walking a fine line between blowing it out and breathing life into it. After a few long minutes, the thin wedges of log began to ignite, the rough splinters crackling and sparkling. I looked around at the faces of the kids—Dev, my niece, and my nephews—waiting patiently, each holding a long stick with marshmallows speared on the ends. Their expressions announced their anticipation but not a lot of confidence in my abilities.

Poking at the weak embers at the bottom of the pile and carefully feeding more twigs into the fire, I silently begged it to come to life. *Please pretty, pink flames, grow and stretch, become hot and yellow and orange. Please.* It was no use. The logs still weren't catching, and my fire was barely more than a few short, weak flames. I was just about to send the kids back into the now dark forest for more twigs, when we heard footsteps approaching our campsite.

Four men appeared around the van, each carrying logs. I recognized them as the men who were enjoying the fire we had envied earlier in the evening. With the briefest of introductions, they set immediately to work on the sad specimen of a campfire I had been slaving over for nearly an hour. Within a few minutes, bright yellow flames were jumping from log to log, the air around us warmed quickly and filled with the crackling of burning wood.

"Your logs weren't dry enough," one of the men explained, and I wondered if he had read the feeling of failure that gripped me. More likely he assumed we had taken the campground wood from under the deck, which we should have known was still wet.

On our last morning, as I drank a mug of freshly percolated coffee in the cool morning air, I felt proud. We had made it through the trip with only minor bumps and scrapes, and a few blood sucking parasites. The kids had fun and the mothers actually had some time to relax. We'd managed cooking on the camp stove, cleaning the dishes, and avoiding wild animals, for the most part. I had proven that moms can camp; I could camp, even if I still couldn't make a proper fire.

Adventures in Travel

ℭ

Despite the warnings and doubts of almost everyone I know, when I knew I was going to be a single parent, I determined that I would not give up my passion for travel. Child or not, I was going to continue going out on the road, to see and experience what the world has to offer. I knew traveling with a child would present challenges, and I knew I'd have to adjust some of my usual travel practices, but I was sure there would be plenty of new experiences along the way.

In my carefree, solo days, I packed as lightly as possible, always aiming to get what I needed into a single backpack style bag that could be carried onto the plane. For longer trips, I researched places to do laundry along the way, rather than packing more clothes. I thoroughly researched public transportation for the destinations, taking full advantage of trains and busses to get around, as well as the occasional ferry.

I planned days packed with adventures and sightseeing, and nights in cheap rooming houses.

With a child in tow, the amount of baggage I had to pack and carry more than doubled. I could no longer manage carry-on, having my hands full just getting Dev on and off the plane, and had to check all our bags. Train hoping was no longer a viable option, and I had to budget for rental cars and European gas prices. I planned quieter days, at a slower pace, and nicer accommodations to lay our heads.

Dev was only a year and a half when I brought him to England, along with my mother and sister. Having extra hands on our first international trip proved useful, as it took the three of us to keep up with him and prevent him from running into the streets or walking off the top of a castle. We learned quickly that we were all happier if we planned time each day to just let him run and climb. And we took full advantage of the stroller to get us to the head of most lines at tourist attractions.

Dinner was a bit difficult in England, as my mother, sister, and I are fans of pub eating. In the countryside, where dining choices were limited, it was never a problem to bring Dev into the pub with us. But in the cities, we weren't able to go to the pubs with child in tow.

Our next international adventure was a long weekend to Paris with my sister, when Dev three years old. Our hotel room was impossibly small, and though we had requested a crib, we ended up just laying the crib mattress on the floor. In the close quarters, sleep was an issue, as Dev talked in his sleep all night long. My sister and I would lay in bed, awake and exhausted, but laughing, listening to the nonsensical conversation coming from my young son.

A life-long dream of mine has always been to go to a Picasso museum, so we made our way across Paris to the museum, Dev in his stroller. Despite the language barrier, we managed to get into the museum, stroller and all, through the handicap access. No sooner had we reached the center of the museum, at the top of a long sloping spiral, when Dev decided to stand up in his stroller and scream at the top of his lungs. No matter what I did or said, I could not get him to stop. Within minutes, a museum docent was beside us, yelling at me in French. I told my sister to take her time, then fighting back tears, my dream crushed, I pushed my son down the ramp and out of the museum as quickly as I could. As soon as we were outside, he calmed down, became down-right cheerful in fact, and chatted away while we waited in the courtyard for my sister. Thankfully, she volunteered to wait with him while I ran through, but I still felt like everyone was glaring at me, asking in French what I was thinking to bring a child into a museum.

Our next adventure was a two-week trip to Ireland, just the two of us, when Dev was almost four. With only a few logistical issues, and a little juggling, we made it out of the airport terminal and into our rental car. I had learned my lessons, and our trip was a balance of planned and free time, all done at a leisurely place. Thanks to the Irish love of children, we were able to eat in pubs and stay in B&Bs. We saw a rainbow every day and were stopped in the road on several occasions by herds of cows standing in the way. This, in fact, was the highlight of the trip for Dev, who loved the fact that a cow almost pooped on the front of the car.

Thinking I was being clever, I planned a two-day castle tour as part of our trip. We saw a dozen or so castles over two days, each in varying states of ruin, several of which we were able to climb in and explore. What more could a young boy ask for, right? On the second night of our castle tour, as my exhausted son slept, his little body curled up in the middle of a queen-size hotel bed, he mumbled, "No more castles. No more castles."

In the summer of 2001, when Dev was four and a half, I received a contract to write a travel guide, and my wanderlust brought us to visit Quebec Province, Canada, almost every weekend for four months. The amount of time we spent on the road that summer pushed the limits of both our tolerance levels.

During one weekend, we found an adorable inn, the romance of which was totally lost with us. Our room came with a four-course gourmet French meal and, I was assured, a meal from their children's menu. The restaurant staff, clearly unsure about the merits of having a four-year-old in the dining room, sat us at the back of the restaurant, and handed me the adult and child's menus.

Making my choices for each course was not a problem, but I grew uneasy quickly as I read through the kid's menu, which turned out to be an abbreviated form of the adult menu, and only two courses. I chose a carrot soup for Dev and a duck dish with mashed potatoes that I hoped he'd believe was chicken. He took a couple sips of the soup but was not impressed. When his main course came, he was even more disappointed. The duck was shaped in dark little triangles—it couldn't have looked less like chicken—and the mashed potatoes were arranged in a stiff, neat tower, which I had to agree was less than appealing. While I had thoroughly enjoyed my mushroom soup, salad, and steak, I was concerned that Dev was not getting dinner.

Though Dev's meal did not come with dessert, mine did, and I let him choose. He picked a selection of homemade sorbets made with fresh fruit from the inn's own gardens and orchards. His eyes brightened as the plate was placed between us. Excitedly, he took a spoonful of one flavor and placed it in his mouth. His lips stretched into a broad smile. "Now this is what I'm talking about," he said loud enough for the diners around us to hear, as well as a passing waitress.

A trip to Moosehead Lake in Maine, when Dev was nearing his teen years, involved coffee and a good book by the lake for me and movies on a laptop for him, moose safaris, hiking, and appetizers for dinner. Dev's plans for swimming and boating were foiled by a cast on a broken wrist, but he was still able to spend some quality time skimming rocks.

As Dev has grown older, our approach to travel has adjusted. We began to discuss our options and decide on destinations together. Whether it's a day away, a long weekend to a lake, or a week-long camping trip, our trips are studies in compromise. And while food, one of Dev's priorities in life, will always remain at the top of the list of issues to work out, we remain easy travel companions.

The End of Playtime

☙

It often takes me by surprise when I look at the little man perched across the room from me. What happened? How did we get here? Who took my little boy; where did he go? It feels like it happened over night, from the darkening shadow of a mustache stretching across his upper lip, which looks like a smudge of dirt he refuses to wash away, to the ever-deepening voice, and his instinctual need to sleep the entire morning away. Intellectually, of course, I know this is a process that's been going on for the past few years, a phasing, morphing of my son as he develops from a boy to adolescent. But it doesn't feel that way. It feels sudden and surprising.

It hit me full force when we decided to start cleaning out Dev's room. For an hour, we pulled out bucket after bucket of old toys and games that had long ago been abandoned and forgotten. Marble tracks, action figures, blocks, Candyland, and remote-control cars, all faded and dust covered.

"It's been a long time since you've played with any of these," I said.

And that's when I had the classic light-bulb-over-the-head brain flash. It wasn't just that he doesn't play with these particular toys any more, he doesn't *play* at all any more—not in the sense of carefree abandon, imagination, and fantasy, the way young children play. I wanted to cry. I felt defeated and depressed over this loss, for myself as well as my son, like someone had stolen a part of him that I knew we'd never get back. I closed my eyes and remembered the honey-haired boy who spent hours every day talking to himself, acting out games he had made up, moving around any objects he could get his hands on, making them characters in his fantasy worlds. When was the last time I had seen him do this? When was the last time he had talked to himself in response to his imagination, rather than the words of a song I would inevitably disapprove of or the events in a video game?

A process of mourning began. The questions I had were at once imperative and ridiculous. How could my son stop playing? Why do we stop playing when we grow up? Why does inventive play turn from something wonderful and developmentally critical, to something immature and un-cool? When does fantasy and imagination turn from magical to embarrassing? Why can't we all just spend our days fantasizing and playing?

When I was about my son's age, wobbling along that

line between being a kid and growing up, I went through an awkward phase when I struggled to define my relationships with my friends and what exactly it was that we did together. I wanted to say, "I'm going out to play with Trudy." But that wasn't right. In some ways, we were still playing, but our games had changed. We were playing at growing up, at mimicking her older sister, becoming women, and catching boys. And, I'm sure, in many ways, this was just as critical to our development as when we were five, playing house, school, and tag. I still remember tripping over my words, as though play had become a curse, the p-word. As if adolescence wasn't hard enough, this inability to define who we were and what we did together was a source of self-consciousness for an entire summer.

At the ever-so-mature age of twelve, my son no longer plays. He games, chills, hangs, shoots hoop, builds (with Legos still), battles, and kicks a ball, but he doesn't play. I started analyzing everything he said, listening for how he was choosing to define his friendships and their activities, my ears ever tuned and waiting for that little p-word. I hold video games partially responsible for this pre-mature decline in playtime. As kids are usually alone when playing video games, they aren't interacting with their peers, and they aren't using their own imaginations or creativity.

In my quest to understand why people give up on play as they grow and mature, I started to wonder why it was that we play at all. Behavioral scientists maintain that play is spontaneous and natural, that many animals exhibit an ability to and enjoyment of play, that it is rare to play in times of stress, and that play is not a means to an end, but the end in-and-of itself. In his book, *The Genesis of Animal Play*, psychologist Gordon Burghardt points out that animals whose parents protect and feed them, such that the young animals are not out searching for their own food or places to hide from predators, are most prone to playfulness. Burghardt argues that play in animals may begin as a way to spend time and use energy, but that play transforms over time into an important developmental tool in which young animals learn about their environment, practice survival skills, and develop social bonds. Dogs, horses, tigers, even octopuses and rats, all play.

It seems to be the overwhelming consensus of the experts that play is a vital part of our development. Plato argued that play was the best type of education for a child. But, it seems, animals don't just stop playing as they grow older. They may play less often as their responsibilities increase, such as hunting and finding shelter for their young, but it doesn't cease all together.

As adult human beings, we throw around the word play, like a self-indulgent act we don't take seriously. Our toys become real cars, boats, and all-terrain vehicles, or sports equipment for tennis, basketball, and softball. And, with rare exceptions, if we're going to let loose and really play, like flying kites, running remote control vehicles, or building sandcastles, we most often do so with the children in our lives, but rarely on our own, just for the sake of it. Psychiatrist Stuart Brown, M.D. says, in his book *Play: How it Shapes the Brain, Opens the*

Imagination, and Invigorates the Soul, "The ability to play is critical not only to being happy, but also to sustaining social relationships and being a creative, innovative person." Play can lead to a longer, healthier, and more fulfilling life. Yet, even in this hyper-health-conscious society, we abandon playtime and all its benefits. As we grow older, fantasy and imagination become things to keep private rather than celebrated as healthy forms of play. Perhaps this is why I enjoy writing fiction, where my imagination can run free and bring life to fantasy worlds. I can still play house, or doctor or post office, but I do it in my mind and on paper instead of acting it out.

As my son runs out the door on a bright and sunny Saturday afternoon, I want to call after him, "play hard, play a lot." Instead, I hold my tongue. Just as I was not ready to give up on play when I was his age, I'm not ready for him to give up on play. I want to bring playtime back into our lives, rather than letting it slip further away.

Play is something we always did because we wanted to, we chose to, not because anyone forced us to. No one paid us to imagine, fantasize, build, and create. It was fun, for the sake of fun, and if we were gaining anything from it, we were blissfully unaware.

Though many adults continue with sports, it is rarely simply for the fun of it, for the sake of play. Most adults who participate in sports, do so as a form of exercise to stay fit and healthy. There is a motive, a purpose, an end goal beyond the game itself, and there's nothing wrong with that, but it's not *play.* Most adults, who do indulge in some play, do so only on special occasions, like when they're on vacation, and do not make it a part of their regularly scheduled life.

Our children learn from our behaviors. When they are young, they learn social rules and behaviors by mimicking adults, playing house. As they reach adolescence, children learn to behave like grown ups by continuing to follow the examples set for them. If adults don't play, how can we expect our older children to play? The challenge then, for parents, is to decide if we will continue to allow the death of playtime, or change the pattern, change the lessons we teach, and make play—true imaginative, fantasy world play—a valuable part of our lives at all ages. I relish the thought of adding play back into my life, for Dev's sake and mine. I gave in too easily at twelve years old, but I don't have to give in at forty-six.

The Gender Thing Revisited

 CB

Being the single mother of a boy has had its challenges from the beginning. I had felt a great sense of accomplishment in making sure he learned how to stand-up pee and helping him decide if he was a boxer, brief, or boxer-brief guy. But, as puberty descended upon us like a thick black cloud, I realized quickly that I was in for the greatest challenges we faced so far. Learning these lessons was a matter of safety, a matter of the future, and lives could be at stake.

The first serious issue of puberty came before I was ready. Dev has always been early on all of his "milestones" of growing up, a trait I attribute to his Mediterranean genes, and body hair was no exception. Before he was even a teenager he had already begun sporting the thick black hairs of a burgeoning mustache, and before he was twelve he was asking to shave.

Dev being an accident-prone child, I was not thrilled at the idea of him using a sharp razor, never mind on his face, or anywhere near such vital parts as his throat and carotid artery. I put the issue off, arguing first that the mustache was not yet thick enough to shave, then that I was worried he'd hurt himself, and finally admitting that I really didn't know how to teach him to shave his face.

"I know how," Dev assured me. "It's not a big deal."

"Maybe I should have Papa show you," I said, thinking my father could handle it. But, when I asked, my father didn't think that was any more necessary than Dev did. They both seemed confident he'd be just fine. My father gave me suggestions on what to buy, which I filed away, and hoped that somehow Dev would forget the idea, and we'd never have to deal with it.

As his twelfth birthday came and went, the cute dusting of dark hairs was beginning to fill in and grow longer. It still didn't look much like a mustache, but its presence was unmistakable.

"You have to let me shave," Dev insisted.

"If you start shaving," I said, "it will come in thicker, and you'll have to keep shaving." I hoped that the thought of this becoming a regular chore, or the thought of even more hair coming in on his lip would deter him.

"It's alright," he said, in the usual way he did whether we were talking about cleaning up a spill or riding his bike in a pounding blizzard.

I was finally forced to express my true reservations.

"I'm nervous about you using a sharp blade on your face. You could cut yourself."

"It's alright," he said again.

For a while, Dev made a point of telling me, on a daily basis, that he needed to shave, and that the hair on his lip didn't look like a mustache, but made his lip look dirty. Finally, tired of his constant pleading and beginning to agree with him that the lip really wasn't looking very good, I took my father's list and went to the drug store. I bought a small can of shaving lotion, a package of disposable razors, and a little white stick that was supposed to help stop the bleeding if he cut himself, though I had no idea how that would possibly work. I had visions of him nicking an artery.

Thrilled to be making this right of passage, Dev disappeared into the bathroom, emerging later with a priceless expression on his face, a mix of bliss, pride, and confidence. Not only was he not damaged or bleeding, I had to admit that he looked good, and he was happy.

With the deepening of his voice, the hint of an Adam's apple beginning to protrude in his neck, and ever-increasing patches of hair appearing under his arms, over his lip, and on his chin, puberty had settled on us like Dorothy's house landing on the Wicked Witch of the East. One afternoon, the day was hot and sunny, as we drove through town, I noticed that my sweet little boy was staring out the window, ogling scantily clad young women, turning his head so far around to look behind us that I wondered if his neck was double jointed.

Don't get me wrong, Dev has always had an eye for the

girls. In kindergarten, he was in trouble almost daily for kissing girls. In first grade he hung a picture of Jennifer Lopez on his wall. But suddenly, it no longer felt like a harmless appreciation; there was the potential for getting into trouble. Girls were sending him text messages at all hours of the day and night, sometimes up to fifty messages a day.

With no father in the house, as always, it fell on me to guide my son through this time. I wanted to rely on my own father, my brother, or a brother-in-law to tell Dev the ways of the world, the birds and the bees, but I knew this was my job. Thankfully, Dev and I have managed to always maintain an open, blunt, and honest line of communication between us.

Thanks to school and the internet, there was not much left for me to explain or teach. At twelve, he knew more about life and sex than I ever did through all of my teen years. Instead, I focused on the bigger picture.

"You need to think about your actions," I said, on more than one occasion. "Be smart. There are always consequences."

"It's alright," he'd always reply, his favorite response, regardless of the question or conversation. "I know."

"Do you want to be a father by the time you're fourteen?" I'd ask. "Because you know I'll make you take responsibility."

"I know," he'd reply. "It's alright."

I looked at him, as he looked at the girls, and fear gripped my heart. *Does he know?* I wondered. *Will it be alright?* The challenges and the consequences would only get bigger, and I hoped that I would be able to steer him through it.

"It's alright," he'd always say, "I know," and I prayed he was right.

An Epilogue of Sorts

୪

Often, I think of my life as books in a series. The first book was my life before Dev came along. It feels like a story I read long ago, the details are fuzzy, and I have to work to recall the events, characters, and plot. The second book has been my life with Dev. It is fresh and clear in my mind, each phase of his life a chapter full of delicious sensory details, action, and emotional appeal. There has been humor and heartbreak throughout the story, but our leading characters look like they will survive, though they may not end up with everything they originally desired.

Reluctantly, I realize that the second book of my life is coming to an end, and a new book is about to start. I don't want this book to end. Each day I try to keep the story going, unwilling to turn the page, mourning the end of one book and the beginning of the next. I sense that the characters in this book will come away from this story strong, confident, and ready to take on the world, but I'm not ready for them to move on just yet.

At the same time, I am excited for what the next book might bring. There is that ever-growing sense of anticipation that a new story brings new adventure, more humor, and more heartbreak, but the possibilities are infinite. There is loss, but there is also the knowledge that there could be gain. And, of course, there is the understanding that the characters will continue into the next book; it's a series, after all. They aren't going away, but they are changing, and their relationships are changing. It's scary business.

I'm not alone facing this new book, this new phase of life. Most of the people I know are at, have recently passed, or are nearing the same point. We are all facing that moment when our children step free of us and enter the world as their own, fully realized and wholly independent human beings. For some parents, it is their first child, their oldest, and the blow is somewhat softened by having another one still at home. For others, it is their last or their only, and there is a feeling of impending doom we can't seem to escape.

On the other hand, like everything else, I am entirely alone in this process, this transition. While other people are talking with their partners and spouses about life with the "empty nest", making plans for what they will do when their child or children are out of the house, I can only ponder the options with myself. It is a lonely proposition in many ways. The possibilities seem at once infinite and severely limited.

I have friends who are enthusiastically embracing grandparenthood in this third book of life. I am not even close to being ready for that. Of course, my second book is not quite finished yet. Dev is only just beginning to launch into his own life, and he is still fairly young, all things considered.

There are times, as there are when reading any good book series, when I want to skip ahead and know what will happen in the next volume. I want to know that Dev will be alright, as he has so often told me he is. I want to know that he will be happy and satisfied with his life, that he'll have love and feel successful. And, of course, I do look forward to having grandchildren. But that book of my life is still closed and unknown to me.

As we wrap up our second tome, we have begun to wrap up this story and prepare for the next. Our conversations, which once focused on practice schedules, sleepover plans, and what movie to see on the weekend, now center on making budgets, paying bills, writing resumes, and the state of the world.

It will be bitter sweet, but I know that I will be satisfied when this second book concludes. I will start the final part of our trilogy with anxious anticipation and confidence, knowing that we have prepared each other for what comes next, as best we can. Though we will be moving on different plot lines, most likely from different home bases, we will continue to have each other, wherever the story brings us.

Some Final Notes

CB

This book has been a labor of love, a long-time in the making. It has been our life together, so far. We've shared it with many people. I could probably fill an entire book just with the number of people I would like to thank for their support and encouragement, in the writing of these stories, the making of this book, and during the pursuit of my writing dream. And the number of people I'd like to thank for the support and help along this road with Dev is even longer. To keep it simple, I will try to focus on those who were instrumental in making this collection a reality.

The amazing women of the former Southern New Hampshire Woman's Writing Group —Laurel Lloyd, Charlene Pollano, Deborah Regan, Martha Walsh, and Sue Wereska — for being a constant source of support, camaraderie, and killer feedback while I wrote these essays, met the deadlines for my column, and made my way into the writing life.

My family, who continue to support me in every way, no matter what direction my fantastical dreams turn me or how often they change direction, and who have been an amazing support for both Dev and me on this wild ride.

Amber Fogg, who started out as a babysitter, so I could sit in a café to write, and who quickly became a part of our family. It would be impossible to ever adequately repay her for all she has been and done for us in this journey.

My many friends who have listened to stories about "the boy", shared in the joys and struggles, and bolstered us immeasurably.

And of course Dev, the love of my life, without whom I would never have had these stories to tell. My life would be unimaginable, unbearably dull, and empty without him.

Made in the USA
Columbia, SC
08 May 2018